Arizona Spring Training Ballpark Guide
A Fan's Guide to the Ballparks of the Cactus League

2011 Edition

Graham Knight

Published by Baseball Enterprises, Inc.
Printed in the USA

First printing: January 2011

ISBN: 1450573061

To contact the author with questions or comments, or if you are a
retailer wanting to place a discounted bulk order, send an e-mail to
grahamak@gmail.com.

AUTHOR'S NOTE

Like their big league brethren, spring training ballparks are dynamic structures. Each year each ballpark undergoes slight modifications, enhancements, or upgrades. While some, and probably most, of any applicable changes are reflected in each ballpark chapter or have no bearing on its content, a limited amount of information may be slightly amiss as a result. Specifically, food items can vary from year to year and what's listed under the "Food For Thought" section may not be available at a particular ballpark this spring. As for team schedules and ticket prices, all information is accurate as of January 23, 2011.

If you find any inaccurate information or think that something is lacking, please feel free to let me know via e-mail at grahamak@gmail.com. This ballpark guide is an annual affair, and next year's edition – like the ballparks themselves – is sure to be slightly different than the 2011 edition.

Thanks for giving me the opportunity to be your Cactus League ballpark guide, and I sincerely hope you find the book useful and your time in Arizona well spent.

- Graham Knight

TABLE OF CONTENTS

INTRODUCTION

Last year, for the first time since its inception, the Cactus League was on equal membership footing with its older, Florida-based spring training counterpart.

The Cincinnati Reds' departure from the Grapefruit League ensured that 15 teams apiece would be training in the (usually) warm climes of Arizona and Florida in 2010... and for the foreseeable future.

That 50/50 split is a stunning turnaround from just two decades ago, when the Cactus League had but eight members and there was talk of its demise. Such talked reached a fever pitch in the wake of the Cleveland Indians' announcement in 1992 that they were leaving Arizona for Florida. Baseball's commissioner at the time, Fay Vincent, didn't mince words when he said, "The Cactus League is struggling. Obviously if teams leave it is not very indicative of a climate where teams are going to want to come."

Obviously, things have changed a lot since 1992. Since then, five teams have relocated to Arizona, the Indians moved back from Florida, and two expansion franchises chose the Grand Canyon State as their spring training grounds, beginning with the Colorado Rockies in 1993.

The relocation trend started in 1998 when the Chicago White Sox left Sarasota, the same Florida city that the Reds abandoned, for Tucson, where the newly minted Arizona Diamondbacks set up shop with the Sox.

Five years later, the Kansas City Royals and Texas Rangers followed the same Florida to Arizona path that the White Sox blazed to jointly train in Surprise; 2009 brought the Indians back and the Los Angeles Dodgers west, thereby leaving old Sunshine State stalwarts Winter Haven and Vero Beach sans the pro sport that the two small Florida towns had long supported each spring.

With the exception of the Dodgers, who wanted to be closer to their fan base, the primary reason behind the exodus of each team from Florida to Arizona has been the new training facilities and ballparks that have sprouted up in the Sonoran Desert, within which each Cactus League team trains.

While the "facilities" - the practice fields, clubhouses, medical/rehab centers, etc. - are of the utmost importance to the teams, the ballparks that anchor the increasingly pricey and grandiose complexes are the focus of the fans...and this book.

The 15 teams that call the Cactus League their winter home utilize just 10 ballparks for their games. That's because five of Arizona's currently used spring training complexes were designed to hold two teams. Along with the five single team use stadiums, all 10 are intimately broken down in their own chapter for you, the fan, who fills them each spring.

Included in this guide is as much information as you'll find about the latest and greatest (and yet to open, as of press time) spring training complex, Salt River Fields at Talking Stick, which lured the Diamondbacks and Rockies *north*, away from Tucson and to the Indian reservation near Scottsdale belonging to the Salt River Pima-Maricopa Indian Community.

The tribes' bucked a trend by privately financing their "Disneyland of baseball," as Diamondbacks President Derrick Hall called the new Salt River Fields, and eschewing the public subsidies that have been responsible for each of Arizona's other green and spring cathedrals. As a result of the Indian Community's generosity, spring training in Arizona is now a Phoenix only affair and Tucson is off the Cactus League map on which it had always been.

Whether, like Salt River Fields, 2011 will be your Cactus League debut or you make the trek to Arizona each spring, this book ensures that you will get the most out of your day at the ballpark, no matter which ballpark you happen to be at on any given day.

So, regardless of if it's shaded seats or autographs that you seek, you'll know where to find each. Furthermore, the cost of tickets and parking are given, all seating sections are described, and the locations of nearby hotels and restaurants are listed, as are the schedules for each team.

From how to get to the ballpark to what's available to eat when you get there to if your seat will have a cup holder to whether that cup can be filled with Coke or Pepsi at the concession stands…it's all here in an easy to read and use format.

CACTUS LEAGUE MILEAGE CHART

	GLE	GYR	MAR	MES	PEO	PHX	SALT	SCT	SUR	TEM
GLE		16	12	32	12	23	35	29	15	24
GYR	16		20	40	26	31	40	37	30	33
MAR	12	20		27	14	15	27	15	17	18
MES	32	40	27		22	10	13	11	47	12
PEO	12	26	14	22		15	31	19	9	16
PHX	23	31	15	10	15		14	4	35	7
SALT	35	40	27	13	31	14		6	38	16
SCT	29	37	15	11	19	4	6		36	10
SUR	15	30	17	47	9	35	38	36		38
TEM	24	33	18	12	16	7	16	10	38	

KEY
GLE = Glendale

GYR = Goodyear

MAR = Maryvale

MES = Mesa

PEO = Peoria

PHX = Phoenix

SALT = Salt River

SCT = Scottsdale

SUR = Surprise

TEM = Tempe

CAMELBACK RANCH
10710 West Camelback Road
Phoenix, AZ 85037

The 2011 season will be the 3rd that the Dodgers and White Sox have jointly trained at the Cactus League's only complex that is operated by its tenants, which makes Camelback Ranch quite the departure from the city-run norm.

LOCATION
The ballpark is on land owned by Glendale that's actually within the city limits of Phoenix. The land was purchased in the 1990s for use as a buffer for the neighboring Glendale Municipal Airport. Eventually, the nearly 500 undeveloped acres close to the spring training complex will be full of shops, restaurants and hotels. But for now, the only significant construction completed in the immediate area is the Camelback Ranch neighborhood that is across the street from the baseball complex.

DIRECTIONS
Take the Loop 101 to the Camelback Road exit (#5) and travel west for about 1½ miles. The stadium is just past the intersection of 107th Avenue and Camelback Road on your right-hand side.

PARKING
The complex has ample parking, 5,000 spaces total, divided up between two lots, neither of which is paved (although there is a paved lot for season ticket holders). The parking lot behind center field is accessed directly from Camelback Road, while the lot to the immediate west of the ballpark is entered via Ballpark Boulevard (aka 111th Avenue).
Cost: Free

Time saving tip for arriving at the ballpark:
When exiting the 101 get into the left lane of the two-lane
highway that heads toward Camelback Ranch so you'll bypass
most of the backed up traffic that is entering the first parking lot
gate. Cruise on by those standing still vehicles in the right lane
to Ballpark Blvd. and turn right. Traffic flows much easier into
the west gate lot that is behind both the first and third base sides
of the stadium and you'll save lots of pre-game time in line by
opting for it.

BALLPARK BASICS
Capacity: 13,000
Opened: 2009
Construction cost: $100 million
Primary architect: HKS Architects

Owned by the City of Glendale and operated by the Dodgers
and White Sox.

First game: The White Sox defeated the Dodgers 3-2 on March 1,
2009 in front of 11,280 fans.

Outfield Dimensions   Phone:
LF: 345' CF: 410' RF: 345'   623-302-5000

BALLPARK OVERVIEW
Camelback Ranch became the largest spring training stadium to
ever open on either coast when it debuted on March 1, 2009.
Capable of holding 13,596 fans, it is one of the few recent new
ballparks not to be built by HOK Sport (now called Populous).
The honor instead went to HKS Architects of Dallas. They
designed the ballpark so that its main entrance is in center field.
A two-acre lake and numerous walking trails made of

decomposed granite were incorporated into the 141 acres of property allotted for the complex, giving it the feel of a park. Interior walls made of stones and wire mesh give the stadium a natural desert look. The Dodgers left 61 years of tradition in Vero Beach behind, abandoning their famed Dodgertown complex for a two-team complex closer to their fan base. The White Sox signed on to be the second team while they were still obligated to fulfill a lease at Tucson Electric Park that ran through the 2012 season. They were able to break that commitment by paying a $5 million buyout. Simply called Glendale Ballpark during much of its construction, on November 20, 2008 it was announced that the entire spring training complex would be called Camelback Ranch. The name was later slightly amended to Camelback Ranch-Glendale at the city's insistence.

Outside the Park

Fans enter the ballpark at street level, the majority of them via trails from the parking lots that lead to the center field gate. There is also a much lesser used entry gate behind home plate.

Sets of ticket windows can be found next to both entrance gates.

Camelback Ranch was designed to fit in with its desert environs, hence its earth tone colors, Afghan pines planted beyond the outfield, and heavy usage of Gabion (stone filled) walls.

Inside the Park

The main concourse wraps around the playing field and is above the seating bowl and berm. It's covered only where it runs beneath the press box and suites.

Both bullpens are cut into the outfield berm near the foul poles. The White Sox pen in very fan accessible in right field, the Dodgers' much less so in left, as berm seating is not available directly above it like it is for the White Sox's.

The stadium has a single scoreboard, an angular looking thing behind the berm in right-center field that features an impressive video board and full line score.

Two souvenir shops, each called Clubhouse Store, carry a decent selection of merchandise for both teams. The shops are located behind home plate and center field, adjacent to each of the ballpark's entrance gates. There's also a Cap Corner in the first base concourse that sells hats for all Cactus League teams.

PRACTICE FIELDS

A dozen practice fields, six for use by each team, are spread out over the Camelback Ranch campus and are separated by a 1,300-foot lake running through the middle of the complex.

The Dodgers' practice fields are located on the eastern side of the campus, where an orange grove also resides. The White Sox's practice fields are on the western half of the campus, where they are in clear view of the cars driving along Camelback Road. Gates for all practice fields open to the public at 9:00 a.m.

SEATING

A whopping 13,000+ fans can be crammed into Camelback Ranch, where stadium-style seats (plastic chairs with backs) make up all of the seating in the grandstand. Lawn seating accounts for the rest of the capacity in the bleacherless ballpark.

SECTIONS & TICKET PRICES

* Ticket prices vary depending on whether the game is classified as "regular" or "premier." Premier games are those versus the Cubs and Diamondbacks, plus the Giants on March 4 and A's on March 18. All other games are considered regular, but prices for regular games go up $2 on game day.

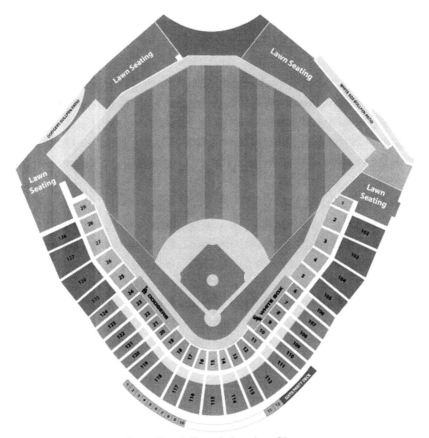

Camelback Ranch Seating Chart

Home Plate Box

Sections 14-16

Seat rows: 1 to 10 in sections 14 and 16; 1 to 8 in section 15

Home Plate Box seats are the priciest non-premium seating a fan can buy in a Cactus League ballpark. They are found in the three as-close-to-field-level-as-you-can-get sections directly behind home plate.

Cost: $42 or $47

Dugout Field Box
Sections 6-13 and 17-24
Seat rows: 4 to 10 in sections 6-10 and 20-24; 1 to 8 in section 11;
1 to 10 in sections 12-13 and 17-19
As their name implies, these seats are directly behind the
dugouts, which are wide enough that five sections of seating are
behind each of them. In 2011, an extra half-dozen sections that
were previously sold as Home Plate Box (sections 11-13 and 17-
19) had their classification changed to Dugout Field Box.
Cost: $37 or $42

Baseline Field Box
Sections 1-5 and 25-29
Seat rows: 1 to 10 in sections 1-2, 5, 25, 28-29; 1 to 8 in sections 3-
4 and 26-27
Each side of the ballpark has five sections of Baseline Field Box
seats, which start just beyond the dugouts and extend down the
left and right field line.
Cost: $28 or $33

Infield Box
Sections 106-124
Seat rows: 1 to 19 in sections 106-108, 112, 118, 121, 123-124; 1 to
22 in sections 109-111, 113-117, 119-120, 122
This massive category of seating comprises the upper two-thirds
of the grandstand that stretches from dugout to dugout. They
have great views of the playing field and its backdrop. Because
they are all within the infield they provide a close to the action
feel, but maybe more importantly they are the closest seats to
the covered portion of the concourse that is the sole respite from
the sun in the sun-drenched ballpark.
Cost: $24 or $29

Baseline Reserved
Sections 102-105 and 125-128
Seat rows: 1 to 19 in sections 102-104 and 126-128; 1 to 21 in sections 105 and 125
The cheap seats aren't exactly cheap in Glendale but at least they come with good views. Called Baseline Reserved, they are the upper two-thirds portion of grandstand seating beyond the dugouts and are positioned behind the Baseline Field Box seats.
 Cost: $15 or $20

Berm Seating
General Admission
The berm starts where the grandstand ends and goes all the way around the outfield, enabling Glendale's grass to hold 3,000 fans.
 Cost: $8 or $13

Handicapped Seating
Handicap accessible seating is available in platforms on the concourse above these sections: 3, 4, 11, 15, 26, 27, 102, 103, 104, 106, 107, 112, 118, 121, 124, 126, 127, and 128. Two other sections - 108 and 123 - have wheelchair accessible platforms above them but are taken up by TV cameras if the game is televised.

VIP seating
The stadium has a dozen suites, a suite-level party deck, and party patios above each bullpen. And then there's the 198-seat Home Plate Club section, which made news during Camelback Ranch's inaugural season for their $90 price tag, the highest in all of spring training. In 2010, the price per Home Plate Club seat was slashed in half and their main perk - access to a complimentary buffet that was behind section 115 on the concourse – was eliminated, along with the complimentary water and sunscreen that were a part of the VIP package.

WHAT YOU NEED TO KNOW BEFORE YOU GO

1. The Dodgers dugout is on the third base side. To make sure you're on the Los Angeles side of the stadium, buy your tickets in sections 16-29 or 116-128.

2. The White Sox dugout is on the first base side. To make sure you're on the Chicago side of the stadium, buy your tickets in sections 1-14 or 102-114.

3. All seats are painted a caramel color (no kidding) but only the exclusive Home Plate Club seats have cup holders, meaning most don't.

4. The protective screen behind home plate extends from sections 11-19 but is barely noticeable to fans sitting behind it.

5. Depending upon which side of the grandstand you sit you have two choices of backdrops. The South Mountains can be seen from the third base side of the ballpark, the higher up and further down the outfield lines the better. Ditto for the University of Phoenix Stadium, which opened in 2006 and is home to the NFL's Arizona Cardinals, on the first base side of the park.

6. Thanks to the 360-degree concourse standing room is plentiful and quite popular in two places: 1) behind home plate, where the concourse is covered by the press box, and 2) in left field, where food and drink rails were installed on the concourse behind the Dodgers bullpen.

7. Most ushers are lenient, some think they're the Gestapo, but for the most part you can relocate yourself to sections with empty seats, especially in the upper half of the grandstand (sections 102-128).

Seats to avoid

There really aren't any. The ballpark has great sightlines throughout.

Camelback Ranch is synonymous with sun, so it's not just the fans in the berm that need to bring their sunscreen as shade is almost non-existent in the grandstand too.

Seats in the shade

The Achilles' heel of Camelback Ranch is that it was built facing the southeast. That orientation is the opposite of every other ballpark in Arizona. What that means in Glendale is that the sun is always beating down on you, instead of retreating behind the grandstand as the game progresses like it does at other Cactus League parks. So you definitely need sunscreen. If you forget to bring some, Coppertone Sport bottles are sold in the gift shops.

Although almost no seats are in the shade, there are a smattering that are. At the usual 1:05 p.m. game starting time consider yourself lucky to be in the last few rows of sections beneath the press box and upper level party deck. Specifically, rows 16 & up in sections 110-113 and rows 20 & up in sections 114-117. Plus by 3:00 all seats in sections 111-114 are shaded. If you really want to be out of the sun, join the throng standing on the concourse above sections 110-122, where cover is provided by the press box and suites.

BUYING TICKETS
There are three ways to purchase tickets for games at Camelback Ranch:
1. Online at www.ticketmaster.com.
2. By calling Ticketmaster at **800-745-3000**.
3. In person. The stadium's box office is open from 10 a.m. to 4 p.m. on Monday through Saturday.

Children
Ages 2 & under get in free and don't require a ticket, although any child without a ticket must share a seat with an accompanying adult.

GAME DAY
Gates open 95 minutes before game time, which is 11:30 a.m. for the typical 1:05 p.m. start.

Food, drink and bag policy
- One bottle of water (opened or unopened) per fan can be brought inside.
- Food items in a small, clear plastic bag (no larger than a one gallon baggie size) can be brought into the stadium.
- Bags up to a maximum size of 16" x 16" x 8" are permitted.

Getting autographs
Players from the Dodgers and White Sox make this an autograph-friendly facility. Numerous players from each team take time to sign before and after games down the outfield lines, between their respective dugouts and the end of the grandstand.

FOOD FOR THOUGHT
Not as good as it could be, but there are plenty of concession stands and carts on the concourse that encircles the ballpark.

The standard fare is joined by pastrami sandwiches, sonoran chicken, three types of sausages (Italian, Polish and the Brat), smoked BBQ and roasted ears of corn. The Dodger Dog made its debut in 2010, and the Vienna Beef Chicago Dog has been available since day one.

SODA AND SUDS

Soft drinks are from the Coca-Cola family and lemonade is in ready supply. Hot days and cold beer go hand in hand and there are plenty of both here. Among the choices on tap in the first two years were Deschutes Mirror Pond, Pyramid Hefeweizen, Fat Tire and Shock Top.

AREA INFO

Glendale is just 10 miles northwest of Phoenix and is an up-and-coming suburb if there ever was one. With a population now in excess of 250,000 residents, Glendale has positioned itself as a major player in the world of sports thanks to University of Phoenix Stadium, which hosted the 2008 Super Bowl and is home to the NFL's Arizona Cardinals and the Fiesta Bowl. The futuristic looking stadium is visible from Camelback Ranch and is just a few miles away on the other side of Loop 101. Hockey's Phoenix Coyotes play at Jobing.com Arena next to the football stadium. The arena anchors the Westgate City Center, the area's impressive shopping, dining and entertainment district.

Travelers' notes

- Two major highways are nearby - the Loop 101 (Agua Fria Freeway) and I-10.
- Phoenix Sky Harbor International Airport is 15.4 miles away.
- Much of the surrounding area is still under development, giving it the feel of a construction zone.

NEARBY HOTELS
Approximate distance (in miles) to the ballpark is listed in parenthesis.

Hampton Inn (3.1)
6630 N 95th Ave
Glendale, AZ 85305
Phone: 623-271-7771

Holiday Inn Express (3.6)
9310 W Cabela Dr
Glendale, AZ 85305
Phone: 623-939-8888

Staybridge Suites (3.6)
9340 W Cabela Dr
Glendale, AZ 85305
Phone: 623-842-0000

Comfort Suites (4.3)
8421 W McDowell Rd
Tolleson, AZ 85353
Phone: 623-936-6000

NEARBY RESTAURANTS
Approximate distance (in miles) to the ballpark is listed in parenthesis.

Subway (1.4)
10685 W Indian School Rd
Avondale, AZ 85392
Phone: 623-772-5701

Wong's Chinese (1.4)
10540 W Indian School Rd
Phoenix, AZ 85037
Phone: 623-877-4123

Ramiro's Mexican Food (1.4)
10720 W Indian School Rd
Phoenix, AZ 85037
Phone: 623-877-8407

Brothers Pizza (1.4)
10720 W Indian School Rd
Phoenix, AZ 85037
Phone: 623-877-3660

LOOKING BACK AT LAST YEAR
It's a good thing wins and losses don't really matter in spring training, as the home teams have done a lot more losing than winning in their two springs in Glendale. After the Dodgers and White Sox each lost 9 of the 15 games in which they were the designated home team in their inaugural year at Camelback

Both the Dodgers and White Sox will play 17 games in 2011 at Camelback Ranch, where an average crowd of 7,635 attended 27 games in 2010.

Ranch, the two teams followed that up by winning a combined 4 games (out of 24) in 2010 against opponents other than themselves (the Sox won 2 of 3 games against the Dodgers). Attendance numbers for both teams remained pretty consistent from year one at the Ranch to year two. The Dodgers averaged 8,893 fans for their games in 2010, a drop-off of 237 from the year prior, to rank 3rd out of the 15 teams that train in Arizona. The White Sox drew a respectable average crowd of 6,280, which was 161 more per game than in 2009 and ranked the Chicagoans 8th in Cactus League attendance.

2010 Dodgers Home Record: 4-9-1
Highest Attendance: 13,583 (vs. Mariners on March 27)
Lowest Attendance: 4,140 (vs. Rockies on March 9)

2010 White Sox Home Record: 3-8-2
Highest Attendance: 13,413 (vs. Cubs on March 19)
Lowest Attendance: 3,440 (vs. Mariners on March 8)

2011 DODGERS HOME SCHEDULE

SUN	MON	TUES	WED	THURS	FRI	SAT
27 Angels	28 White Sox	1	2 Royals	3	4 Giants	5 Reds
6	7	8	9 Mariners	10 Padres	11	12
13 White Sox	14	15 Rangers	16	17 D-backs	18	19 Brewers
20	21 A's	22 Cubs	23	24 Rockies	25	26
27 Indians	28	29	30	31		

The game on March 4 starts at 7:05 p.m.

All other games start at 1:05 p.m. local time.

For the full Dodgers spring training schedule, see page 173.

2011 WHITE SOX HOME SCHEDULE

SUN	MON	TUES	WED	THURS	FRI	SAT
27	28	1 Brewers	2	3 Mariners	4	5
6 Royals	7 Indians	8 Rockies	9	10	11 Cubs	12 Rangers
13	14 Padres	15	16 Giants	17	18 A's	19
20 Dodgers	21	22	23 Dodgers	24	25 D-backs	26 Angels
27	28 Reds	29	30	31		

The game on March 18 starts at 4:05 p.m.

The game on March 25 starts at 7:05 p.m.

All other games start at 1:05 p.m. local time.

For the full White Sox spring training schedule, see page 167.

GOODYEAR BALLPARK

1933 South Ballpark Way
Goodyear, AZ   85338

The 2011 season will be the second that Goodyear's ballpark has operated as the anchor of a two-team complex. In its debut season of 2009, Goodyear Ballpark hosted just the Indians. A year later the facilities were expanded to accommodate their Ohio counterparts and the Reds made their Cactus League debut in 2010, leaving Sarasota, FL to do so.

LOCATION

Goodyear Ballpark is the centerpiece of the city's ambitious ballpark village master plan, a 240-acre mixed-use development that will one day include offices, shops, restaurants, and a hotel and conference center. But before all of that is completed the ballpark will be most notable for its proximity to the Phoenix Goodyear Airport, where numerous large commercial airliners sit idly by while waiting to be disposed of.

DIRECTIONS

Take I-10 to the Estrella Parkway exit (#126) and travel south for about two miles. The ballpark will be on your left, just past Yuma Road.

PARKING

The combination of paved parking lots and grass fields that surround the ballpark can hold up to 3,000 vehicles.
 Cost: $5

BALLPARK BASICS
Capacity: 10,311
Opened: 2009
Construction cost: $108 million
Primary architect: HOK Sport

Owned and operated by the City of Goodyear.

First game: The Giants defeated the Indians 10-7 on February 25, 2009 in front of 4,181 fans.

Outfield Dimensions	Phone:
LF: 345' CF: 410' RF: 345'	623-882-3120

BALLPARK OVERVIEW
Sprawling over 103 acres, the $108 million Goodyear Ballpark and Recreational Sports Complex is the most expensive spring training venue ever built. It hosts two teams that hail from Ohio, as the Reds joined the Indians in 2010. In 2009, Cleveland had the Goodyear facilities to themselves while Cincinnati was finishing up a 12-year tenure in Sarasota, FL. Designed by HOK

Sport, the main stadium seats 10,311 fans, many of whom enjoy fantastic views of the nearby Estrella and White Tank Mountains. Built on what was for over seven decades privately owned farmland, the ballpark blends in with its southwestern landscape thanks to its earth tone colors. Its most noticeable item of decor is the baseball spire that greets fans near the home plate entrance. Standing 60' 6" tall, the fiberglass and steel sculpture by artist Donald Lipski was designed and installed at a cost of $450,000 to the City of Goodyear, which owns, operates and retains naming rights to the ballpark.

Outside the Park
The backside of the scoreboard serves as the stadium's welcome billboard and is positioned adjacent to the center field entrance gate.

Fans enter the ballpark at street level through one of four gates, each named after their location: home plate, first base, third base and center field (which is actually in left-center field).

Nine ticket windows are located next to the home plate gate, which is designed to be the ballpark's main entrance, and another four are located in the ticket booth adjacent to the center field gate.

Inside the Park
The concourse completely wraps around and is open to the playing field. It's covered only where it runs beneath the press box and suites.

Both bullpens are in front of the left field berm, the Indians' closest to the foul pole.

The stadium's only scoreboard is located behind the berm in left-center field and has a video board and electronic line score.

A Kids Zone can be found in the right field corner and includes inflatable games and a mini baseball field.

Mini souvenir stands are scattered about the ballpark while the main team shop is found just inside of the main entrance behind home plate.

PRACTICE FIELDS

The Recreational Sports Complex contains a dozen full-sized practice fields. The Indians and Reds have year-round use of two apiece, with the other eight controlled by the City of Goodyear outside of February and March.

While not next door to the ballpark, the development complexes for both teams are within walking distance of it. The separate complexes are where the Indians' and Reds' major leaguers practice and minor leaguers train.

The actual addresses for the teams' complexes are 2601 S. Wood Blvd. for the Indians and 3125 S. Wood Blvd for the Reds. The Indians' complex is closer to Goodyear Ballpark and plenty of dedicated parking spaces are on each side of Wood Blvd., ensuring a short walk to each.

Practice field gates open daily at 9:00 a.m. Prior to the beginning of Cactus League games, the teams generally practice from 9:30 a.m. to 12:30 p.m.

SEATING

Stadium-style seats (plastic chairs with backs) make up all of the seating in the grandstand. The rest of the stadium's patrons sit in the outfield, either on the berm or in the party deck in right field.

SECTIONS & TICKET PRICES

Club Seating
Sections 106A, 106B and 107A
Seat rows: Q to Y in all sections
Club seating is not on a club level, but instead mixed in with box seats and even with third base. The reason why they are allowed to be allotted as "club," a designation that makes them the most expensive "regular" seats in the house, has to do with the roof that covers each of the three sections, thereby making the 316 padded club seats the only ones in the ballpark to enjoy such an amenity.
Cost: $27

Infield Box
Sections 106-118
Seat rows: A to M in section 106; E to M in section 107; E to Y in sections 108-109; A to Y in sections 110-111; A to Z in section 112; A to Y in sections 113-114; E to Y in sections 115-117; A to Z in section 118
Found in the portion of the grandstand that surrounds the perimeter of the infield, there are 13 Infield Box sections and they contain a total of 3,957 seats, which easily makes them the largest category of seating that's available in the ballpark.
Cost: $23

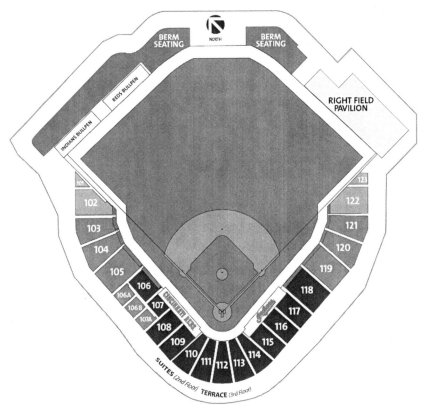

Goodyear Ballpark Seating Chart

Outfield Box

Sections 103-105 and 119-121

Seat rows: A to Y in sections 103-105 and 119; A and D to Y in section 120; A to B and D to Y in section 121

Another section with a logical name, Outfield Box seats are quite simply situated down the outfield lines, where three such sections are along each outfield line and hold a total of 2,610 seats.

Cost: $18

Outfield Reserved

Sections 101-102 and 122-123

Seat rows: R to Z in section 101; A to Y in section 102; F to Y in section 122; T to Y in section 123

Tapering upwards at the edge of each end of the grandstand are a pair of sections eloquently referred to as Outfield Reserved. Besides their price, the best part about them is the grandstand is sloped inwards so that the 868 seats they contain are all facing the infield.

Cost: $12

Berm

General Admission

Up to 1,500 people are able to sit on the lawn that extends from the left field foul pole to right-center, where the berm is elevated a handful of feet higher than the berm on the left field side of the ballpark.

Cost: $8

Handicapped Seating

Handicap seating is available on the concourse, in row Z, above every seating section except 101, 112 and 118. There are a total of 176 accessible seats.

VIP seating

Six suites make up the ballpark's only upper level seating and include all you can eat ballpark food, just like the Right Field Pavilion party deck does. Tickets in the party pavilion, which has tables on a tiered balcony, are sold individually for $30 while the cost to rent a suite is $750. Atop the suites is the Terrace, a rooftop area that can hold up to 90 people (at $35 per) and was designed for groups, but if space is available day of game tickets are sold to individuals for just $15. At field level, the Premium Field Boxes retail for $27. Those seats - there are

256 total - are simply the first row of seats in sections 102-106 and 118-122.

WHAT YOU NEED TO KNOW BEFORE YOU GO

1. The Indians dugout is on the first base side. To make sure you're on the Cleveland side of the stadium, buy your tickets in sections 112-123.
2. The Reds dugout is on the third base side. To make sure you're on the Cincinnati side of the stadium, buy your tickets in sections 101-111.
3. All seats in the stadium are below the concourse and have cup holders.
4. Rows I and O are skipped in all sections.
5. The further down and higher up the outfield lines you sit the better your view of the nearby mountain ranges, the Estrellas from left and the White Tanks from right.
6. Standing room is plentiful on the 360-degree concourse, which includes food and drink rails behind the last row of seats in many sections.
7. Ushers are not restrictive when it comes to moving about the ballpark's grandstand.

Seats to avoid

The beauty of a newer ballpark is that there's generally not a bad seat in the house. That holds somewhat true in Goodyear, where some of the best seats in the house - those directly behind the dugouts - have an annoying protective screen in front of them. Try to sit above row G in sections 108-109 and 115-116 to minimize the annoyance. Additionally, Outfield Box and Reserved ticket holders will not be able to see into the outfield corner closest to them, as the grandstand curves in such a way that it obstructs views of the playing field near the foul pole. While that's only a potential nuisance a couple times per game, the tarp that's stationed in front of section 105 is a nine inning

Many of the good seats in the grandstand are shaded thanks to the press box, but the ballpark's berm is completely sun-drenched.

issue for fans in the first two rows there. As a result, the seats in rows A and B in section 105 are the worst in the ballpark, even though they are padded and at field level.

Seats in the shade

There are plenty, as the press box casts a shadow upon many of the seats in sections 111-114 (and most of them by the end of the game). But for a sure thing, sit in the three sections of Club Seating, compromised of sections 106A, 106B and 107A, where all seats are covered by a roof. If opting for the slightly less expensive Infield Box seats behind the plate, shade is guaranteed at the beginning of a 1:05 p.m. game in rows X & up in section 111, rows S & up in section 112, rows R & up in section 113, and rows Q & up in section 114 (except for seats 1-4).

Mountain ranges provide a pleasing backdrop for fans sitting down the outfield lines. The Estrellas are shown here, while the White Tank Mountains are visible from the seats pictured.

BUYING TICKETS

There are three ways to purchase tickets for games at Goodyear Ballpark:

1. Online at www.ticketmaster.com.
2. By calling Ticketmaster at **800-745-3000**.
3. In person. The stadium's box office is open from 9 a.m. to 5 p.m. on Monday through Friday and from 10 a.m. to 2 p.m. on Saturday. Also, fans in Cleveland can purchase spring training tickets at the Progressive Field box office. Ditto for fans in Cincinnati at the Great American Ball Park box office.

Children

Children under the age of 3 do not need a ticket while ages 3-12 can get in for half price in a buy one, get one half-off ticket promotion that applies to three sections: Outfield Box, Outfield Reserved and Berm. For each regularly priced ticket purchased in those sections a ticket for a child may be bought at half price.

GAME DAY
All gates open an hour and a half before game time.

Food, drink and bag policy
- Only a single factory-sealed water bottle is allowed inside. If the bottle has already been opened you can't bring it in. Unopened juice boxes are allowed to be brought inside for children.
- The only food permitted is unopened snacks and baby formula.
- Bags can be brought inside, provided they are smaller than 16" x 16" x 8".

Getting autographs
Because players enter the field through doors in the right field wall they don't have to walk close to the fans in the stands, which isn't a good setup for those wanting to get autographs. Furthermore, the protective screen attaches to the ends of the dugouts, effectively serving as a barrier there between fans and players or coaches. Despite these obstacles not all hope is lost. When Cleveland is playing in Goodyear, before the game begins some Indians players will sign down the right field line. Visiting players who sign do so down the left field line, near the tarp. When the Reds play at home, the inverse is true, meaning Cincy players sign down the left field line and the visitors in right. The pattern here is the right field line is a much more bountiful place to get autographs than the left field line.

FOOD FOR THOUGHT
There's plenty of food options, but not much that is out of the ordinary. The most original choices actually involve an old standby, the hot dog. Visit Hot Dog Nation behind home plate to select from a jumbo, New York, Chicago, Arizona, Cleveland or Cincinnati-style wiener. A Mexican grill is in the third base

plaza, a pizza place on the first base plaza, and freestanding Philly cheesesteak stands can be found near each. Other eating options of interest abound down the outfield lines, where BBQ nachos and sandwiches are served in right field and Cincy's favorite chili (Skyline) is served atop a Coney from a concessionaire along the left field line.

SODA AND SUDS

Beer on tap is plentiful in both location and variety, with the tried and true (Coors and Miller Lites) mixing in with the new (Deschutes, New Belgium and Sierra Nevada brews). The soft drink of choice is Coca-Cola.

AREA INFO

Although it is the smallest city in the Cactus League, Goodyear is one of the fastest growing cities in Arizona, expanding from just 18,911 residents in 2000 to 59,508 in 2008. The land on which the spring training complex was built was for many decades privately owned farmland. Now it is being transformed into an area rich with commercial, recreational and residential development. Many nearby homes and shops have already been completed, but the area will be a construction zone for years to come.

Travelers' notes
- The closest Interstate, I-10, is 2 miles away.
- Phoenix Sky Harbor International Airport is 20.5 miles away.
- The entire city is safe, befitting of a place that was named as one of just 10 All-America cities for 2008.

NEARBY HOTELS
Approximate distance (in miles) to the ballpark is listed in parenthesis.

Best Western (2.3)
55 N Litchfield Rd
Goodyear, AZ 85338
Phone: 623-932-3210

Holiday Inn Express (2.4)
1313 N Litchfield Rd
Goodyear, AZ 85395
Phone: 623-535-1313

Residence Inn (3.4)
2020 N Litchfield Rd
Goodyear, AZ 85395
Phone: 623-866-1313

Super 8 (3.5)
840 N Dysart Rd
Goodyear, AZ 85338
Phone: 623-932-9622

NEARBY RESTAURANTS
Approximate distance (in miles) to the ballpark is listed in parenthesis.

Subway (2.2)
525 N Estrella Pkwy
Goodyear, AZ 85338
Phone: 623-882-8181

Brothers Pizza Express (2.2)
525 N Estrella Pkwy
Goodyear, AZ 85338
Phone: 623-925-9401

Native New Yorker (2.2)
530 N Estrella Pkwy
Goodyear, AZ 85338
Phone: 623-882-0022

Chili's (2.4)
1371 N Litchfield Rd
Goodyear, AZ 85395
Phone: 623-535-4222

Trivia Tidbit
The Goodyear complex was originally designed to host only the Indians. But when the Reds' situation in Florida became unsettled the city agreed to convert it into a two-team facility, which cost an extra $32 million and required the purchase of another 48 acres.

The Reds will play 17 games in 2011 at Goodyear Ballpark, where for the third straight spring the Indians are scheduled to play 18.

LOOKING BACK AT LAST YEAR

The Reds' inaugural season as a member of the Cactus League was less than stellar. From the mediocre win-loss record to a dead-last attendance ranking (4,170 per home game), Cincinnati's desert debut was pretty much a dud. The Indians did much better on the diamond but were almost as dismal at the box office, as their average home crowd of 4,374 ranked them 14th out of the Cactus League's 15 teams.

2010 Indians Home Record: 10-3-1
Highest Attendance: 6,647 (vs. Diamondbacks on March 27)
Lowest Attendance: 2,271 (vs. Padres on March 10)

2010 Reds Home Record: 6-7-3
Highest Attendance: 7,693 (vs. Mariners on March 19)
Lowest Attendance: 2,017 (vs. Royals on March 8)

2011 INDIANS HOME SCHEDULE

SUN	MON	TUES	WED	THURS	FRI	SAT
27 Reds	28	1 Dodgers	2	3	4 Rockies	5 White Sox
6	7	8 D-backs	9 Padres	10	11 Mariners	12 Angels
13	14 A's	15 Brewers	16	17	18 Rangers	19
20 D-backs	21	22	23 Royals	24	25	26 Giants
27	28 Cubs	29 Reds	30	31		

The games on March 18 & 26 start at 7:05 p.m. The start time for the March 12 game is 2:05 p.m. The March 29 game begins at 12:05 p.m. All other games start at 1:05 p.m. local time.

For the full Indians spring training schedule, see page 169.

2011 REDS HOME SCHEDULE

SUN	MON	TUES	WED	THURS	FRI	SAT
27	28 Indians	1	2 White Sox	3 Dodgers	4	5
6 Cubs	7 Brewers	8	9	10 Giants	11	12
13 Angels	14	15	16 Royals	17 Indians	18	19 Rockies
20	21 Mariners	22 A's	23	24 Rangers	25 Padres	26
27 D-backs	28	29	30	31		

The games on March 3 & 16 start at 7:05 p.m.

All other games start at 1:05 p.m. local time.

For the full Reds spring training schedule, see page 168.

HOHOKAM PARK

1235 North Center Street
Mesa, AZ 85201

The 2011 season will be the Cubs' 47th in Mesa, where they have trained for all or parts of the previous six decades in two stints that have spanned 1952-65 and 1979 to present.

LOCATION

Hohokam Park is in a residential area of Mesa, directly across the street from the City of Mesa Cemetery.

DIRECTIONS

From Phoenix:

Take Loop 202 east to the McKellips Road exit (#12). Turn right on McKellips then right on North Center Street. The stadium will be on the left. The driving distance from Loop 202 (aka the Red Mountain Freeway) is 1.8 miles.

From the south (Chandler/Tucson):

Use Highway 60 (aka Superstition Freeway), exiting at Country Club Drive (exit #179). Travel north on Country Club for about 3.4 miles then turn right (east) on Brown Road. Proceed to North Center Street and take a left. The ballpark is just ahead on the right.

PARKING

There are 3,000 spaces at the stadium, the bulk of which are in grass fields that are used for youth soccer on non-game days. The fairly sizable (by spring training standards) paved lot is for season ticket holders and is designated as Lot A. Just like in Chicago, neighborhood parking is available. It's necessary in Mesa thanks to the big crowds that the Cubs draw. The benefit to parking at homes belonging to local residents is much easier

exiting upon game's end. Stadium and neighborhood parking are priced the same.
Cost: $5

BALLPARK BASICS
Capacity: 13,074
Opened: 1997
Construction cost: $18 million
Primary architect: HOK Sport

Owned by the City of Mesa and operated by the Mesa HoHoKams.

First game: The Cubs beat the Mariners 6-2 on February 28, 1997, in front of 8,804 fans.

Outfield Dimensions	Phone:
LF: 340' CF: 410' RF: 350'	480-644-4451

BALLPARK OVERVIEW
Hohokam Park is best known for its large crowds. Its seats and berm are regularly filled to capacity, and capacity in Mesa is larger than at any other spring training ballpark. As such, the Cubs own the single season (203,105 in 2009) spring training attendance record. There's no doubt the Cubs are the draw, as the stadium's bland tan stucco exterior leaves a lot to be desired. The expansive interior is utilitarian in design, with the upper grandstand providing wonderful views of the surrounding mountain ranges. Just like at Wrigley, the fans make Hohokam a wonderful experience and every game one of them is picked to lead the crowd in the signing of "Take Me Out to the Ballgame." Referred to interchangeably as Hohokam Park and Hohokam

Stadium, the current structure opened in 1997 on the same spot as the original Hohokam Park, which was razed and rebuilt following twenty years of use. The stadium is named after the Mesa HoHoKams, an influential local civic organization that has been the booster of spring training baseball in Mesa since 1951. There's no word yet on whether the stadium's name will be retained when its replacement opens a couple miles away in a couple of years. Mesa's voters approved a city referendum on November 2, 2010, to provide the majority of funding ($99 million) for a new training complex that will anchor the Cubs' vision of Wrigleyville West, a concept that will surround the new ballpark, tentatively scheduled to be ready in time for 2013 spring training, with privately-funded dining, shopping and entertainment options.

Outside the Park

Fans enter the ballpark at street level through one of multiple gates. Gate A is behind center field and is the main berm entrance, Gate B is in the left field corner, Gate C is behind third base and is the most used entrance, Gate D is on the first base side of home plate, and Gate E is behind first base.

The majority of ticket windows are next to Gate C, although there is a cash only window near both Gates B and D. Ticket lines get backed up at Gates B and C, but not D. If you don't need to use a credit card head there to reduce your time waiting in line.

Inside the Park

The main concourse is behind and covered by the grandstand. Banners of Cub greats hang from its walls. An interior concourse completely encircles and is open to the playing field.

The bullpens are tiered in right field with the Cubs' closest to the playing field. Only a chain link fence separates fans from the visitors' bullpen.

The stadium's main scoreboard is a 32-foot tall behemoth that stands behind the berm in left field. It has a video board and electronic line score. Mini scoreboards are attached to the façade of the two Upper Deck Cafes.

The playing field is named in memory of Dwight W. Patterson, the founding member of the Mesa HoHoKams.

A pair of team shops, both named the Cubbie Hole, can be found behind home plate and third base, respectively.

PRACTICE FIELDS

The Cubs have a practice field just beyond the ballpark's center field wall. The team's minor leaguers practice and play on the four fields found within Fitch Park, which is located a half-mile south of Hohokam Park at 160 East 6th Place. The major league Cubs practice at Fitch Park until they begin playing Cactus League games. When the big league Cubs are there in February, Fitch Park's gates are usually unlocked by 8 a.m.

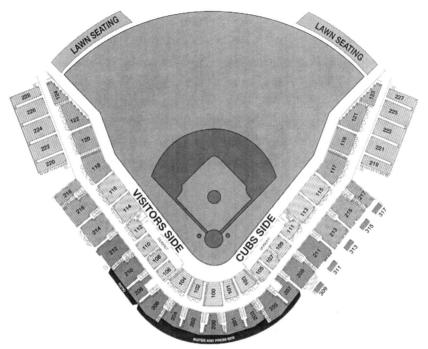

Hohokam Park Seating Chart

SEATING

Hohokam Park has a capacity of 13,074 and since the Cubs are the most popular team in Arizona that number is often exceeded, although in 2010, when the team averaged "only" 10,892 fans for their 14 home games, the Cubs drew crowds of over 13,000 just twice.

SECTIONS & TICKET PRICES

* Ticket prices vary depending on whether the game is classified as "regular" or "premium." Premium games are those played in March on Friday, Saturday and Sunday, plus the Thursday (March 24) game against the White Sox.

Field Box

Sections 100-116

Seat rows: C to P in section 100; C to L in sections 101-104; F to P in sections 105-110; F to L in sections 111-112; A to L in sections 113-116

The 17 sections of Field Box seating are filled with green chair back seats, with the majority of them between the dugouts. Those in sections 113-116 are the exceptions, as they are just beyond the dugouts.

Cost: $28 or $30

Terrace Box

Sections 200-212

Seat rows: AA to LL in sections 200-204; AA to PP in sections 205-212

Although they aren't the closest to the field, the 13 sections of Terrace Box seats are probably the best in the house for both views and shade. They are comprised of the same green chair back seats found in the Field Box sections but have a slightly lesser price since they are above the aisle.

Cost: $26 or $28

Field Reserved

Sections 117-124

Seat rows: A to L in sections 117-122; G to N in sections 123-124

Field level bleacher seats with backs make up the four sections on each side of the ballpark that extend down the left and right field lines to the foul poles.

Cost: $21 or $23

Note: A single row (P) at the top of sections 123 and 124 contains traditional stadium seating instead of bleachers.

Terrace

Sections 213-218
Seat rows: AA to PP in all sections
A less comfortable version of the Terrace Box seats, the half dozen sections of Terrace seating are comprised of bleachers with backs that are just beyond the infield. They are priced the same as Field Reserved seats, although the Terrace seats offer shade and generally a better view, considering their elevation above the ballpark's interior aisle.
Cost: $21 or $23

Note: A single row (QQ) at the top of sections 213, 215-218 contains traditional stadium seating instead of bleachers.

Patio Bleachers

Sections 219-228
Seat rows: AA to RR in all sections
These are the freestanding sets of bleachers found down each outfield line and they are filled with bleacher seats with backs.
Cost: $17 or $19

Grandstand

Sections 309, 311, 313, 315, 317
Seat rows: A to C in all sections
In 2009, these odd-numbered only sections of padded bleacher seats were added to the patio above 200-level seats on the first base side of the stadium.
Cost: $15 or $17

Trivia Tidbit

Former Mesa Mayor Keno Hawker served as an usher in the right field bleachers during his mayoral tenure, which ended in 2008.

It's not the biggest berm at a Cactus League ballpark, but the one found at Hohokam Park is often the most crowded thanks to a scarcity of seats available in the grandstand.

Lawn

General Admission

The berm extends from foul pole to foul pole in the outfield and can hold 2,575 fans, more of whom can fit on the larger right field lawn than the less spacious left field lawn.

Cost: $8 or $9

Handicapped Seating

Handicap accessible seating is available on railed in platforms on the aisle at the top of sections 101-104 and 111-122. Handicap seating is also available in areas above sections 209, 212 & 214.

VIP seating

There are two outdoor patios, one on each side of the press box. The third base patio is adjacent to an indoor skybox. The ballpark has six luxury suites. The Budweiser Party Deck in right field can hold up to 250 people.

WHAT YOU NEED TO KNOW BEFORE YOU GO

1. The Cubs dugout is on the first base side. To make sure you're on the home side of the stadium, buy your tickets in any odd numbered section.
2. Rows I and O are skipped in all 100-level sections, while rows II and OO are skipped in all 200-level sections.
3. Seats do not have cup holders.
4. An aisle cuts through the middle of the grandstand. All 100-level seats are below the aisle while all 200-level seats are above it.
5. The protective screen behind home plate extends from sections 100-104 and doesn't obstruct views of those sitting behind it.
6. Fans in even numbered 200-level sections (third base side) have a nice view of the Superstition Mountains.
7. The outfield berm is a standing room haven, specifically on the larger right field berm. There's also plenty of room to stand on the aisle between 100- and 200-level seats.
8. Ushers are very friendly. All members of the Mesa HoHoKams, they will generally let you sit in sections for which you don't have a ticket as long as there is availability. But given the Cubs' drawing power that's not often.

Seats to avoid

They're not necessarily bad seats, but those in sections 117-124 are aluminum bleachers and the higher the section number the further away your seat will be from home plate. For example, sections 123 and 124 are very close to the foul poles. Some seats in the 300-level bleachers are obstructed by poles. Although padded and shaded, the spaces that are sold as Grandstand (or Grandstand Reserved) are some of the worst seats you'll find at any spring training ballpark. You're better off sitting in the berm.

Seats in the shade

There are plenty here. The stadium's trellised roof casts shade upon all rows in sections 200-207, 209, 211 and 213. Most seats in sections 208, 210, 212, 214 and 216 are in the shade, with all seats in those sections shaded by 1:45.

BUYING TICKETS

There are three ways to purchase tickets for Cubs games at Hohokam Park:

1. Online at www.cubs.com.
2. By calling Tickets.com at **800-905-3315**. The ballpark's box office can be reached at **480-964-4467**, but callers to that number will only get to hear a recorded message of general ticketing information.
3. In person. Box office hours are 9 a.m. to 4 p.m. on Monday through Friday.

Children

Ages 3 & under get in free so long as they sit in adult's lap (if in the grandstand; the lap rule doesn't apply to the berm).

GAME DAY

Gates open at 10:30 a.m. but the berm remains closed until batting practice is over.

Food, drink and bag policy

- Food cannot be brought into the stadium, but one sealed bottle of water per person is permitted.
- Bags allowed inside can't exceed 16" x 16" x 8" in size.

Getting autographs

Simply put, this is not a good park to obtain autographs in. Much of the Cubs' batting practice takes place before gates open, limiting fan access to them. Occasionally a Cub player will sign near the tarp close to their dugout before the game, but with tunnels to the clubhouses for both teams located in the dugouts players can easily avoid fans.

The best thing to do is to wait until after the game is over, when many Cubs players will sign autographs once they've showered and changed into street clothes. The place to be is near the exit door of the Cubs' clubhouse at the end of the first base grandstand, from which players emerge in route to their parking lot in the right field corner. To get there, players walk through a closed off section of the concourse inside of the stadium and fans gather along the route in front of the appropriately named Clubhouse Cafe. This is the epicenter of autograph activity inside of Hohokam Park, and it's found directly behind the freestanding bleachers down the right field line.

Away games
When the Cubs play road games they generally take batting practice at Hohokam Park then bus over to wherever they are playing. Ballpark gates in Mesa will be open so Cubs fans can watch the team take BP, which happens between 10 and 11 a.m. Ironically, fans can't watch the Cubs' full batting practice when they are playing at home, as gates to the ballpark don't open until halfway through it, which is an upgrade over seasons prior to 2011, when the Hohokam gates didn't open until just after the team had finished hitting.

FOOD FOR THOUGHT
Although not overly creative, the food is actually pretty good. The biggest issue is that concession stands are behind the grandstand and sold out crowds lead to long lines that will often force you to miss an inning. If you like hot dogs, the Chi-Town Dog (onions, mustard, sport peppers, sweet relish, tomatoes) or

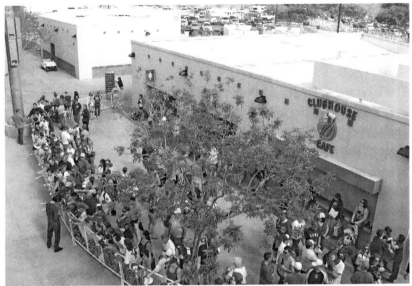

Head to the Clubhouse Cafe after the game - not for food specials, but for autographs from Cubs players exiting their nearby clubhouse.

the Mesa Dog (chili, cheese, fritos, jalapenos) are worth the wait behind home plate at Hot Dog Nation. But mainly you'll find tried and true menu items (pizza, pulled pork BBQ, nachos), although the trailer serving up Iowa breaded pork tenderloins is original.

SODA AND SUDS
Pepsi is the cola of choice. Old Style beer, sold at Wrigley Field since 1950, is also available at Hohokam Park. So too is plenty of beer on tap, with Bud and Bud Light available pretty much everywhere and lesser known brands (like Land Shark) scattered throughout the park.

AREA INFO
Although Mesa is the third largest city in Arizona, the area surrounding the stadium is pretty much summed up by the cemetery across the street from it. There's just not a lot

The Cubs will play 17 games in 2011 at Hohokam Park, where they went 7-6-1 in 2010 before an average crowd of 10,892.

happening. Your time is better spent enjoying the recreational offerings of Phoenix or the upscale shopping and dining found in Scottsdale. Both cities are about 10 miles away. If you like art, the Mesa Arts Center houses five galleries. Baseball fans should make the short drive to the Arizona Museum for Youth, where an exhibit called Play Ball: The Cactus League Experience details the history of the Cactus League. The museum is just 1.9 miles from Hohokam Park and is open Tuesday through Saturday, from 10-4.

Travelers' notes

- The closest major highway, the Loop 202, is less than 2 miles away.
- Phoenix Sky Harbor International Airport is 11.9 miles away.
- The area surrounding the stadium is as safe as it is boring.

NEARBY HOTELS
Approximate distance (in miles) to the ballpark is listed in parenthesis.

Marriott (1.3)
200 N Centennial Way
Mesa, AZ 85201
Phone: 480-898-8300

Best Western (1.7)
250 W Main St
Mesa, AZ 85201
Phone: 480-834-9233

Travelodge (1.8)
22 S Country Club Dr
Mesa, AZ 85210
Phone: 480-964-5694

NEARBY RESTAURANTS
Approximate distance (in miles) to the ballpark is listed in parenthesis.

Native New Yorker (0.45)
318 E Brown Rd
Mesa, AZ 85201
Phone: 480-464-4383

The Dirty Drummer (0.5)
1211 N Country Club Dr
Mesa, AZ 85201
Phone: 480-834-6371

Cindy's Arizona Cafe (0.85)
124 E McKellips Rd
Mesa, AZ 85201
Phone: 480-655-1349

Royal Thai Grill (0.95)
321 W McKellips Rd
Mesa, AZ 85201
Phone: 480-733-9025

LOOKING BACK AT LAST YEAR
As usual, the Cubs were the top draw in the Cactus League, averaging 10,892 per home game, of which there were only 14 due to one rainout. The Giants got in their full allotment of 15 home games in Scottsdale, thereby edging the Cubs (155,819 to 152,493) in total home attendance. On the field, the Cubs fared

much better in Arizona (16-12-3) than they did upon returning to Chicago (75-87).

2010 Home Record: 7-6-1
Highest Attendance: 13,462 (vs. Padres on March 27)
Lowest Attendance: 7,496 (vs. A's on March 4)

2011 CUBS HOME SCHEDULE

SUN	MON	TUES	WED	THURS	FRI	SAT
27 A's	28 Brewers	1	2	3 Rangers	4	5 Padres
6 Dodgers	7 Angels	8	9 Royals	10 Indians	11	12 Reds
13	14	15 Rockies	16	17	18 Reds	19
20 Giants	21	22	23 A's	24 White Sox	25 Mariners	26
27 Rockies	28	29 D-backs	30	31		

All games start at 1:05 p.m. local time.
For the full Cubs spring training schedule, see page 166.

MARYVALE BASEBALL PARK

3600 North 51st Avenue
Phoenix, AZ 85031

The 2011 season will mark the 14th year that the Brewers have trained in the Phoenix neighborhood of Maryvale.

LOCATION

Maryvale Baseball Park is in the western-most city limits of Phoenix. The 56-acre complex is found amongst dense commercial development in the city's Maryvale neighborhood.

DIRECTIONS

Take 1-10 to the 51st Avenue exit (#139) and travel north for two miles. The stadium will be on the left, in a highly visible spot after Thomas and before Indian School Roads.

PARKING

The stadium has a sizable parking lot next to it. Paved spaces are available on a first-come, first-served basis and are the domain of the early to arrive tailgate crowd. Once the large paved lot fills up, cars are routed to the grass field between right field and 51st Ave. And when really large crowds are expected, the nearby Wal-Mart shopping center sets aside some spaces in the eastern edge of its parking lot, which is staffed by Brewers personal.
Cost: $6

Trivia Tidbit

Maryvale was originally envisioned as a two-team complex, with the Chicago White Sox being the other team. The Sox instead opted for the two-team complex that opened in Tucson the same year as Maryvale Baseball Park.

BALLPARK BASICS

Capacity: 10,000
Opened: 1998
Construction cost: $25 million
Primary architect: Ellerbe Becket

Owned and operated by the city of Phoenix.

First game: The Padres beat the Brewers 8-4 on February 27, 1998 in front of 3,102 fans.

Outfield Dimensions	Phone:
LF: 350' CF: 400' RF: 340'	623-245-5555

BALLPARK OVERVIEW

Maryvale Baseball Park is elegantly simple and fan-friendly. Noted for its openness, the ballpark doesn't have a true exterior facade. Instead, white iron gates and beige stone form the perimeter. The ballpark's signature exterior sign sits high atop white iron staging, beckoning fans to the open plaza adjacent to its main entrance down the right field line. Plenty more white wrought-iron can be found inside. It's used to make up the trellised roof that covers the concourse. That roof is supported by white suspension bridge-style cables. Everything else is painted blue, including the sleekest looking press box you'll ever see. The recessed playing field is framed by the berm and trees. Although it's the only Cactus League facility from which you can't readily spot a mountain range, it may be the most pleasant place to watch a ballgame in Arizona, where a few Milwaukee traditions have been brought west. Notable among them are the Klement's Sausage Race and the playing of "Roll Out the Barrel" following the 7th inning stretch. The ballpark was built on land donated by the area's developer, John F. Long, and named after the neighborhood it resides in. Mary was the name of Long's wife, hence the name Maryvale.

Outside the Park

Fans enter the ballpark at street level. The main and easily most used entrance is Gate A in right field. Two other gates exist, but aren't open every game: Gate B behind third base and Gate C further down the left field line.

Ticket windows are on both sides of the ballpark, but the only ones that are always open are the half dozen to the immediate left of Gate A in right field. There are also two next to the barely used Gate B in left field.

Inside the Park

The concourse is above the seating bowl, where it's covered by a trellised roof, and is open to the playing field that it completely encircles.

Bullpens are cut into the berms down each outfield line - the Brewers in right, visitors in left. Both are fan accessible.

The stadium's only scoreboard is located behind the berm in left-center field and features a line score along with basic game information (balls, strikes, outs) and a panel that lists the name, number and position of the player at-bat.

Two small souvenir shops are set up on the third base side of the ballpark, one in a trailer, but the main team shop, called the Fan Zone, is in the right field corner, just inside the main entrance gate.

PRACTICE FIELDS
The Brewers' training complex and minor league facility is directly behind the ballpark, on the home plate side. Its official address is 3805 N. 53rd Avenue. The five practice fields within the complex are named after former Brewer greats, one each for Cecil Cooper, Rollie Fingers, Paul Molitor, Don Sutton and Robin Yount.

The gates to the practice fields open early (circa 7:00 a.m.) to let the grounds crew in. Fans are welcome inside the complex early too, but there's no point in getting there before 9:00 a.m. Show up prior to then and there is little to do other than watch the grass grow or, more precisely, get cut.

SEATING
Maryvale Baseball Park has a capacity of 10,000, a number that is not often reached as the Brewers are one of the least popular teams training in Arizona. In 2010, the team averaged 5,310 fans for their 15 home games, with the ballpark being at least half full for just seven of them.

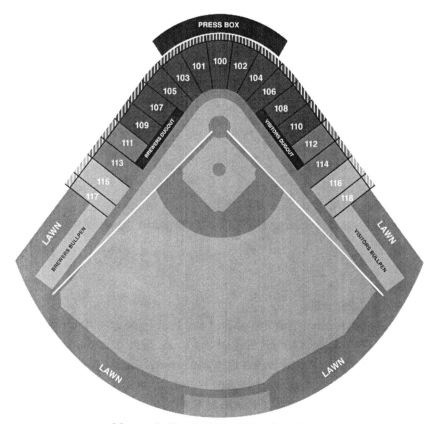

Maryvale Baseball Park Seating Chart

SECTIONS & TICKET PRICES

Field Box

Sections 100-110

Seat rows: C to Z in section 100; A to Z in sections 101-106; F to Z in sections 107-110

The best seats in the house are the only true seats in the house. The 11 sections of field box seating are the sole stadium seats in the ballpark. Bleachers and berm make up the rest of Maryvale's seating options.

 Cost: $22

Infield Reserved

Sections 111-114

Seat rows: F to Z in sections 111-112; A to Z in sections 113-114

Four sections of bleachers with backs that are close to the dugouts.

Cost: $16

Outfield Reserved

Sections 115-118

Seat rows: A to Z in all sections

Four sections of bleachers with backs beyond the dugouts.

Cost: $13

Lawn

General Admission

The berm extends from the end of the first base grandstand around the outfield to the end of the third base grandstand. The berm is steeply sloped in the outfield – no Cactus League ballpark features a greater incline – and fans can stand directly behind the outfield wall so long as they don't lean against it.

Cost: $8

Handicapped Seating

Found in railed off areas on the concourse behind every section except 109 and 110. There is also a handicapped platform in right-center field.

VIP seating

None at all. Bob Uecker would be proud.

WHAT YOU NEED TO KNOW BEFORE YOU GO

1. The Brewers dugout is on the first base side. To make sure you're on the home side of the stadium, buy your tickets in any odd numbered section.
2. Rows I and O are skipped in all sections.
3. Seats do not have cup holders.
4. The protective screen behind the batter extends from sections 100-104 but is barely visible to fans sitting behind it.
5. Lots of great standing room viewpoints are available on the 360-degree concourse and berm.
6. The ushers in Maryvale are as lenient as they come. On days that crowds are sparse you can sit where you like when you like regardless of what your ticket says.

Seats to avoid

None. The stadium's design is simple, yet flawless. There are no obstructions. But don't sit in the outfield berm if hearing the stadium's public address system is important to you. The sound doesn't travel very well out there.

Seats in the shade

Fans seeking relief from the always present Arizona sun should sit on the first base side of the ballpark. For the typical 1:05 start the berm above the Brewers bullpen down the right field line is completely in the shade thanks to the position of the sun and the trellised roof above the concourse. The upper half of every odd numbered section, plus sections 100 and 102, are a haven for shade from rows P and up. By 2:30 shade has enveloped most of the seats below the press box, which casts its shadow down upon sections 100-104. Much of the third base side of the ballpark remains sunny throughout the game, with shade finally creeping down its upper rows near game's end. The bottom line is sit in the upper half of any first base seating section and you won't have much need for sunscreen.

The ballpark's unique trellised roof protects fans standing on the concourse and casts shade upon many sitting in the stands.

BUYING TICKETS

There are three ways to purchase tickets for Brewers games at Maryvale Baseball Park:

1. Online at www.brewers.com.

2. By calling the ballpark's box office at **623-245-5527**. Fans can also purchase spring training tickets from the Miller Park ticket office by calling **1-800-933-7890**.

3. In person. Box office hours are 9 a.m. to 5 p.m. on Monday through Saturday and from 11 a.m. to 3 p.m. on Sunday.

Children

Ages 2 & under get in free and do not require a ticket.

GAME DAY

Gates open approximately an hour and a half before game time, occasionally earlier. The Brewers take batting practice on the field before the gates open and often the visiting team's bus doesn't arrive until about 45 minutes before first pitch. So there's not much point of being inside the stadium when gates officially open at 11:30 a.m. unless you like to watch the grounds crew do their job.

Food, drink and bag policy
- Unopened bottles are allowed inside, cans are banned.
- Food can be brought into the stadium.
- Bags up to a maximum size of 16" x 16" x 8" are permitted.

Getting autographs
All players enter the field through a tunnel next to the Brewers bullpen down the right field line. That's an unfortunate setup, as it effectively serves as a barrier between player and fan.

Pre-game autographs are often more plentiful from the visiting team. Many visiting players will sign down the left field line, between their dugout and bullpen. Visiting team fans should head to sections 114, 116 and 118 about 30 minutes before first pitch. There's not a lot of autograph activity on the Brewers side. Your best bet to snag one is by hanging out in the section (113) next to the home dugout.

Fans will often have more luck getting autographs during and after the game. The reason you'll see a throng of people gathered on the concourse down the right field line near the clubhouse is because some players will sign at the fence there after they have been removed from the game. About 20-30 minutes following the game, especially early in the spring, a handful of Brewers will make their way from the Major League clubhouse to the Minor League clubhouse by walking through the crowd outside of the ballpark. They're not hard to miss, as they will be wearing cleats and carrying their equipment.

The Sausage Race
Just like in Milwaukee, the Klement's Sausage Race takes place before the home half of the sixth inning. The five costumed

Pictured from left to right, the Polish, Chorizo, Bratwurst, Italian and Hot Dog sign autographs the inning after they run the traditional Klement's Sausage Race.

sausages then sign autographs and pose for pictures a short time afterwards on the concourse near section 117.

FOOD FOR THOUGHT

It wouldn't be a Brewers game without Klement's bratwursts. They're available throughout the ballpark, along with Klement's Polish sausage and hot dog. Otherwise, there aren't many specialty food items. Those that do exist can be found at tents set up on the concourse behind home plate, where the most unique offering in past years has been the wok fired soba noodles.

SODA AND SUDS

Coke is the soda of choice and the beer is a no-brainer. Miller products reign supreme, with Miller Lite and the High Life readily available on tap. So too is another Wisconsin brew, Leinie's Sunset Wheat.

The Brewers will play 17 games in 2011 at Maryvale Baseball Park, where they went 8-6-1 in 2010 before an average crowd of 5,310.

AREA INFO

Maryvale was once a nice neighborhood. But those days are long gone. To be politically correct, the ballpark is now in an economically depressed section of Phoenix. Essentially, you go to Maryvale, watch the game and leave, although you do have the option of eating at one of the nearby restaurants. To be fair, Maryvale is nowhere near being a slum. It's just a neighborhood where inglés is a second language and you don't want to be after dark.

Travelers' notes

- The closest Interstate, I-10, is 2 miles away.
- Phoenix Sky Harbor International Airport is 8.3 miles away.
- The ballpark is a safe haven in an area noted for its safety concerns. There's a reason the Brewers' team hotel is 14 miles away in Glendale.

NEARBY HOTELS
Approximate distance (in miles) to the ballpark is listed in parenthesis.

La Quinta Inn (1.7)
4929 W McDowell Rd
Phoenix, AZ 85035
Phone: 602-595-7601

Motel 6 (1.7)
1530 N 52nd Dr
Phoenix, AZ 85043
Phone: 602-272-0220

Red Roof Inn (1.8)
5215 W Willetta St
Phoenix, AZ 85043
Phone: 602-233-8004

Super 8 (2.2)
1242 N 53rd Ave
Phoenix, AZ 85043
Phone: 602-415-0888

NEARBY RESTAURANTS
Approximate distance (in miles) to the ballpark is listed in parenthesis.

Sizzler (0.35)
5060 W Indian School Rd
Phoenix, AZ 85031
Phone: 623-247-5524

Peter Piper Pizza (0.35)
4105 N 51st Ave
Phoenix, AZ 85031
Phone: 623-247-5100

New China Buffet (0.4)
4105 N 51st Ave
Phoenix, AZ 85031
Phone: 623-245-3535

Denny's (0.4)
4120 N 51st Ave
Phoenix, AZ 85031
Phone: 623-247-4195

LOOKING BACK AT LAST YEAR
The Brewers followed up a superb spring in 2009 at Maryvale Baseball Park (14-1-2 record) with a slightly better than average one in 2010, when they drew a total of 79,651 fans, an average of 5,310 per home game, which ranked the Brewers 11th out of 15 teams in the Cactus League.

2010 Home Record: 8-6-1

Highest Attendance: 9,994 (vs. Angels on March 19)

Lowest Attendance: 3,034 (vs. Mariners on March 8)

2011 BREWERS HOME SCHEDULE

SUN	MON	TUES	WED	THURS	FRI	SAT
	28 Giants	1	2 Cubs	3 A's	4	5 Angels
6	7	8 Dodgers	9	10 Rockies	11 A's	12 D-backs
13 Royals	14	15	16	17 White Sox	18	19
20 Reds	21 Rangers	22 Padres	23	24	25 Indians	26 Mariners
27 White Sox	28 Padres	29	30	31		

All games start at 1:05 p.m. local time.

For the full Brewers spring training schedule, see page 174.

PEORIA SPORTS COMPLEX
16101 North 83rd Avenue
Peoria, AZ 85382

The 2011 season will mark the 18th year that the Mariners and Padres have jointly trained in Peoria at the Cactus League's first two-team complex.

LOCATION
The 145-acre Peoria Sports Complex is at the heart of the city's entertainment, retail and dining core. Upscale apartment and office buildings round out the surrounding mixed-use development, all of which are in the shadows of the Loop 101.

DIRECTIONS
Take 1-10 or I-17 to Loop 101 and exit at Bell Road (exit #14). Travel east a very short distance and then turn right onto N 83rd Avenue. The stadium is about a half mile ahead on your left. Turn onto Paradise Lane if you want to park behind the outfield. Take either of the next two streets (Stadium Way or Mariners Way) if you want to park behind the main grandstand.
Note: Loop 101 is also referred to as the Agua Fria Freeway.

PARKING
A plethora of paved parking is on each side of the stadium, 2,700 spaces in total. The parking lots are split into east (outfield) and west (home plate).
Cost: $5

Trivia Tidbit
Peoria is just the second spring training home that San Diego and Seattle have ever had. Prior to relocating to Peoria, the Padres trained in Yuma and the Mariners in Tempe.

BALLPARK BASICS
Capacity: 11,333
Opened: 1994
Construction cost: $32 million
Primary architect: HOK Sport

Owned and operated by the City of Peoria, with game day
volunteer assistance provided by the Peoria Diamond Club.

First game: The Mariners defeated the Padres 7-4 on March 2,
1994 in front of 4,395 fans.

Outfield Dimensions	Phone:
LF: 340' CF: 410' RF: 340'	623-773-8700

BALLPARK OVERVIEW
The Peoria Sports Complex is nothing if not a trend-setter. Built
on what was once barren desert land, it was the first spring
training facility designed to be shared by two teams. The
stadium also had the dual purpose of becoming the economic
catalyst for development in Peoria. It was very successful in that
regard and all new Cactus League projects since have followed
Peoria's two-team complex blueprint. Made with sandstone
shaded concrete and blue steel, the stadium in Peoria introduced
the modern outfield spanning berm and 360-degree concourse to

spring training fans. The backdrop is dominated by buildings built in the same earth tone colors as the stadium, plus palm trees and distant mountain vistas. The stadium was constructed early enough in the 1990s that the concourse was built behind the grandstand. Diamond-shaped plaques displayed atop the facade of the press box recognize the winners of the Spring Training Rookie of the Year award, which has been presented annually since 2002 by the Peoria Diamond Club to the top first year Padres or Mariners player based on their performance at games played in Peoria. Until Camelback Ranch-Glendale opened, the Peoria Sports Complex was the only spring training venue not to be named ballpark, park, field or stadium. Its name instead highlights the complex's 12 full-sized practice fields, four practice infields, and other baseball training facilities.

Outside the Park

The backside of the scoreboard serves as the stadium's welcome billboard, but is visible only to fans who enter the east (outfield) parking lot.

Fans enter the ballpark at street level through one of four gates, depending on where they park. Gates A and B are on the stadium's west (home plate) side. Gates C and D are in the outfield, accessed from the east parking lot. The left field entrance (Gate C) is easily the least congested of all four, although starting in 2010 it will not be open every game.

Ticket windows can be found both behind home plate, between Gates A and B, and the outfield, close to Gate D.

Inside the Park

A continuous concourse runs behind the grandstand and above the berm. It allows fans to completely encircle the stadium.

Both bullpens are cut into the outfield berm near the foul poles - the Mariners' in left, the Padres' in right.

The stadium's only scoreboard is located behind the berm in left-center field and features a video board and electronic line score.

The Kid's Zone behind the first base grandstand has a wiffle ball infield that's one-third the size of a Major League diamond. Additionally, there's an inflatable "Home Run Derby" that lets kids practice their hitting, while "kids" of all ages can get their fastball clocked at the speed pitch station.

A pair of team shops are located a short distance from each other behind home plate (adjacent to Gates A and B). Souvenir stands are also open along the first and third baseline concourses and next to the center field concession stand across from Gate D.

PRACTICE FIELDS
The training complexes for both teams are adjacent to the main stadium, running parallel to the first base line. Gates for the practice fields open to the public at 9:15 a.m. and remain open until early afternoon.

Fans heading to the Padres' practice facilities should park in the stadium's east lot, accessed via Paradise Lane. Fans wishing to watch Mariners practices and pre-game preparations should park in the west parking lot, best entered from Mariners Way.

SEATING
The stadium's grandstand holds 6,105 chair back seats, and all of them are painted blue. Bleacher benches without seat backs are found down each outfield line, totaling 1,728 seats. The spacious berm can hold up to 3,500 people.

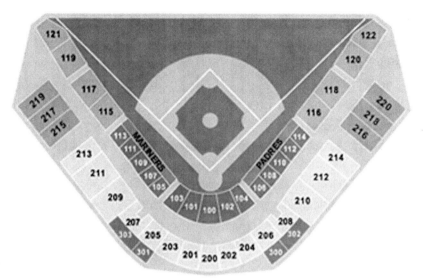

Peoria Sports Complex Seating Chart

SECTIONS & TICKET PRICES

Infield Box
Sections 100-114
Seat rows: A to M in section 100; A to H in sections 101-104; E to M in sections 105-114
These are the choices seats in the house and they ring the infield, extending from dugout to dugout in the lower half of the grandstand.
 Cost: $23

Club Seating
Sections 300-303
Seat rows: 1 to 4 in all sections
Two sections of open-air club box seats flank either side of the press box. All seats are padded and shaded. Club sections offer separate restrooms, concessions and the option of wait staff.

They are walled off from the rest of the grandstand so fans must access them via stairs or through the lobby staircase or elevator.
Cost: $21

Upper Box
Sections 200-214
Seat rows: AA to KK in sections 200-208; AA to PP in sections 209-214
Located behind the Infield Box, from which they are separated by a mid-level concourse, are the Upper Box sections. These seats are just as good as their lower box counterparts, hence the small price discrepancy between the two.
Cost: $19

Outfield Box
Sections 115-122
Seat rows: A to H in all sections
Close to the playing field but not angled towards the infield are the Outfield Box seats, which begin where the dugouts end and extend more than midway down each outfield line.
Cost: $17

Bleachers
Sections 215-220
Seat rows: AA to PP in all sections
A three section set of freestanding bleachers is found down each outfield line in what would be otherwise open space behind the Outfield Box seats. The bleachers lack backs and are the only seats that are overpriced, given what you get.
Cost: $12

Lawn seating is cheap and plentiful, as Peoria's berm can hold 3,500.

Outfield Berm
General Admission
Spanning the entire outfield, Peoria's lawn is packed with more families than any other in the Cactus League, partly because of the price but also because it's a good place to stretch out and watch the game.
 Cost: $6

Handicapped Seating
Handicap accessible seating is available in platforms cut into the top of sections 101-104 and 115-122. The Club section also offers limited accessible seating.

VIP seating
The Red Hook VIP Deck above the right field bullpen is available to groups of 20 to 100. For approximately $41 per person, tickets in the tent-covered deck include all you can eat ballpark fare. Existing tickets may be upgraded to this area

(without the free buffet) on game day if the Hook Deck is not booked by groups. Suites must be booked in advance. They are found within the same structure behind home plate that holds the press box. Each of the stadium's 8 suites holds a dozen people and rents for $500 per game.

WHAT YOU NEED TO KNOW BEFORE YOU GO

1. The Mariners dugout is on the third base side. To make sure you're on the Seattle side of the stadium, buy your tickets in any odd numbered section.
2. The Padres dugout is on the first base side. To make sure you're on the San Diego side of the stadium, buy your tickets in any even numbered section.
3. An aisle cuts through the middle of the grandstand. All 100 level seats (Infield and Outfield Box) are below the aisle, while 200 and 300 level seats (Upper Box, Bleachers and Club Seating) are above it.
4. Rows I and II are skipped in their respective sections.
5. The only seats that have cup holders are those in the Infield Box and Club Seating sections.
6. The protective screen behind the batter extends from sections 100-104 but does not obstruct views of those sitting behind it.
7. Standing room is generally limited to the berm.
8. Ushers allow fans to move freely about the ballpark, only occasionally checking ticket stubs in the Infield Box sections behind and between the dugouts.

Seats to avoid
The Bleachers have no seat backs and that's generally not fun (or comfortable).

Seats in the shade
This ballpark gets a lot of sun but its tiny trellised roof was built more for aesthetic purposes. The only fans that will benefit with

the shade it provides sit in rows JJ and up in sections 200-214 or the Club seats in sections 300-303.

BUYING TICKETS

There are three ways to purchase tickets for games at the Peoria Sports Complex:

1. Online at www.tickets.com, www.mariners.com or www.padres.com.
2. By calling Tickets.com at **800-677-1227**.
3. In person. The stadium's box office is open from 9 a.m. to 5 p.m. on Monday through Friday and from 10 a.m. to 2 p.m. on Saturday.

Children

Ages 2 & under are admitted free but are required to sit on an adult's lap if in the grandstand.

GAME DAY

All gates open approximately an hour and a half before game time. That's 11:30 a.m. for a 1:05 p.m. start and 5:30 p.m. for a 7:05 p.m. start.

Food, drink and bag policy

- Sealed bottles of water can be brought inside the stadium. So too can empty plastic/sport bottles and unopened single serving juice boxes.
- Paper lunch bags containing food may be brought into the stadium.
- Backpacks and other bags are allowed up to a maximum size of 16" x 16" x 8".
- Elevated lawn chairs are not permitted, although fans in the bleachers are allowed to bring in small backed stadium seats (chairs in which the seat bottom rests directly on a surface).

Players from both teams sign plenty of autographs for fans gathered in the right field corner in an area known as Autograph Alley.

Getting autographs

Neither the Mariners nor Padres take batting practice inside the stadium prior to games, opting instead to hit on their practice fields. Visiting teams generally hit in their home park before busing to Peoria. That all ads up to minimal activity inside the stadium before the game starts, when autograph opportunities and limited to sections nearest where the players stretch in the 20 minutes or so before game time.

Peoria is an autograph Mecca during and especially after the game, as fans can get very close to the team clubhouses in the right field corner. All players exit the field through a gate there and walk beneath a bridge. Located beneath the right field bridge, a gravel path leads to "Autograph Alley," a landscaped area complete with artificial grass and hearthscape stone benches where the only thing separating fans from players is a blue wrought iron fence. Fans congregate there while players walk by. Lots of them sign during the game (after they've been taken out) and a whole slew afterwards. The visiting team's bus will also be stationed in that area, backing into place near the end of the game. It's best to position yourself along the fence in a place where you're not blocked from players' views by the bus as they enter and exit the clubhouse.

FOOD FOR THOUGHT
A dazzling array of specialty food options can be found in the Power Alley, a spacious and festive area behind the third base grandstand. One important exception is the grille behind home plate that serves up a select number of items that are popular in San Diego and Seattle. A specially priced kid's meal (PB&J or hot dog, chips and soda) can be found at the concession stand by the wiffle ball field, while Baja fish tacos are cooked fresh to order for fans willing to make the trek out to right-center field. Seemingly anything else a food connoisseur could ever want, from gyros to burritos, can be found in the Power Alley, making Peoria the pride of the Cactus League when it comes to dining.

SODA AND SUDS
Pepsi is the cola of choice and some microbrews are featured. Like all ballparks during spring training, beer on tap is plentiful and varies from stand to stand.

AREA INFO
The best way to sum it up is there's a little bit of everything nearby. From an ice skating rink to a movie theatre to dining, drinking and shopping establishments galore, the Peoria stadium district has become a year-round destination. It's a fine example of a ballpark spurring mixed-use development with spring training fans and local residents both benefiting.

Travelers' notes

- There are three major highways a short drive away - Loop 101, I-10 and I-17.
- Phoenix Sky Harbor International Airport is 17.4 miles away.
- The stadium is one of the most fan-friendly in spring training. It's also one of the safest.

NEARBY HOTELS

Approximate distance (in miles) to the ballpark is listed in parenthesis.

La Quinta Inn (0.1)
16321 N 83rd Ave
Peoria, AZ 85382
Phone: 623-487-1900

Hampton Inn (0.25)
8408 W Paradise Ln
Peoria, AZ 85382
Phone: 623-486-9918

Residence Inn (0.3)
8435 W Paradise Ln
Peoria, AZ 85382
Phone: 623-979-2074

Comfort Suites (0.35)
8473 W Paradise Ln
Peoria, AZ 85382
Phone: 623-334-3993

NEARBY RESTAURANTS

Approximate distance (in miles) to the ballpark is listed in parenthesis.

PF Chang's China Bistro (0.1)
16170 N 83rd Ave
Peoria, AZ 85382
Phone: 623-412-3335

Chick-Fil-A (0.1)
16657 N 83rd Ave
Peoria, AZ 85382
Phone: 623-878-0885

Cheesecake Factory (0.1)
16134 N 83rd Ave
Peoria, AZ 85382
Phone: 623-773-2233

Red Robin (0.25)
16233 N 83rd Ave
Peoria, AZ 85382
Phone: 623-334-4600

The Mariners and Padres will each play 17 games in 2011 at the Peoria Sports Complex, where an average crowd of 7,144 attended 28 games in 2010.

LOOKING BACK AT LAST YEAR

In a sign of things to come during the regular season, the Padres fared well and the Mariners poorly in the 14 games each played as the home team in Peoria in 2010. As usual, Seattle outdrew San Diego. The Mariners' average home crowd of 8,597 ranked them 4th out of the 15 teams that train in Arizona. Notably, their March 28th game against the Cubs drew 13,629, which is the single-game Cactus League attendance record heading into 2011. Meanwhile, the Padres ranked 10th in attendance by drawing 5,691 fans per home game.

2010 Mariners Home Record: 4-9-1
Highest Attendance: 13,629 (vs. Cubs on March 28)
Lowest Attendance: 4,263 (vs. Indians on March 9)

2010 Padres Home Record: 9-4-1
Highest Attendance: 10,497 (vs. Dodgers on March 19)
Lowest Attendance: 2,497 (vs. Rockies on March 8)

2011 MARINERS HOME SCHEDULE

SUN	MON	TUES	WED	THURS	FRI	SAT
27 Padres	28	1 Rangers	2	3	4 Reds	5 Indians
6	7	8 Giants	9	10 Angels	11	12 A's
13	14 Cubs	15	16 Brewers	17	18 D-backs	19
20 Padres	21	22 White Sox	23	24 Royals	25 Dodgers	26
27 Rangers	28 Rockies	29	30	31		

The games on March 16 & 25 start at 7:05 p.m.

All other games start at 1:05 p.m. local time.

For the full Mariners spring training schedule, see page 178.

2011 PADRES HOME SCHEDULE

SUN	MON	TUES	WED	THURS	FRI	SAT
27	28 Mariners	1	2 Rockies	3 D-backs	4	5
6 A's	7 Royals	8	9 Reds	10	11 Giants	12
13 Indians	14	15 Angels	16	17 Rangers	18	19 Cubs
20	21 White Sox	22	23 Reds	24	25	26 Dodgers
27	28	29 Brewers	30	31		

The games on March 7, 11, 17 & 21 start at 7:05 p.m.

The game on March 29 starts at 12:05 p.m.

All other games start at 1:05 p.m. local time.

For the full Padres spring training schedule, see page 176.

PHOENIX MUNICIPAL STADIUM

5999 East Van Buren Street
Phoenix, AZ   85008

The 2011 season will be the 30th consecutive that the A's have trained in Phoenix, a tenure that ranks third among all teams in the Cactus League. Only the Cubs and Giants have been in their current locations longer.

LOCATION

Phoenix Municipal Stadium straddles the city limits of Tempe and Phoenix. The welcome signs for each municipality can be seen on Priest Drive directly behind the ballpark, which is bordered by Tempe office buildings and the red rock buttes of Phoenix's Papago Park.

DIRECTIONS

Take Loop 202 to the Priest Drive exit. Go north and the stadium is about a mile away at the intersection of Priest and Van Buren Street.

PARKING

A paved lot across the street from the stadium is your only option. The lot is a big one and is connected to the stadium by a pedestrian bridge above Priest Drive.
 Cost: $5

Trivia Tidbit
The first home run ever hit at Phoenix Muni was a 425-foot shot by Willie Mays, who cleared the center field fence during the stadium's inaugural game, which was attended by Commissioner Ford Frick.

BALLPARK BASICS
Capacity: 8,500
Opened: 1964
Construction cost: $891,380
Primary architect: Unknown

Owned and operated by the city of Phoenix.

First game: The San Francisco Giants defeated the Cleveland
Indians 6-2 on March 8, 1964 in front of 8,582 fans.

Outfield Dimensions   Phone:
LF: 345' CF: 410' RF: 345'   602-392-0074

BALLPARK OVERVIEW
Phoenix Muni, as the stadium is most often called, is the only
holdover left from the Cactus League of yesteryear after its
counterpart in Tucson, Hi Corbett Field, played host to its 64th
and final spring training season in 2010. Built well before
amenities were in vogue, or considered necessary, the Valley's

oldest stadium opened the year the Polo Grounds was demolished, which explains why light poles from that historic New York ballpark ended up in Phoenix. That fact is one of many that are written into the cement blocks that make up the stadium's concourse. History and location are Muni's two best assets. The stadium is most noted for its splendid outfield backdrop, which features the famous red rock formations of neighboring Papago Park. Desert brush is found beyond the left field wall, a stark contrast to the lush berms newer ballparks have. Cactus is a common sight near the stadium's main entrance, which is notable for its baseball covered canvas sunscreens. The desert setting theme is adhered to inside the stadium as well, thanks to inlaid stones that adorn the base of the main grandstand, which is covered by a wavy concrete roof. Originally completed for about $890,000 in 1964, the stadium underwent an $8 million renovation 40 years later that modernized it some, but the original charm has been left intact.

Outside the Park

Fans enter the ballpark at street level through one of three gates. The main entrance is behind third base, which is where the pedestrian overpass leads fans to. A lesser used gate is in left field. The right field gate, which is actually directly behind home plate, is the least congested.

The ticket windows are located next to the third base entry gate.

Inside the Park

Part of the concourse is behind the grandstand, but a larger portion of it is open to the playing field (from the dugouts to the foul poles).

Both bullpens are in foul territory down the outfield lines - the A's in right, visitors in left.

The stadium's only scoreboard is in right-center field and features a line score along with basic game information (balls, strikes, outs, name of player at-bat).

Two small souvenir shops are midway down each outfield concourse while the main team shop is found behind the grandstand between home plate and third base.

PRACTICE FIELDS
The A's hold their workouts in the main stadium and/or on a practice field that is directly behind right field (and mostly obscured from public view).

The team's minor league training complex is 2 miles away at the Papago Baseball Facility, which is found within the confines of Papago Park at 1802 North 64th Street.

To get to the Papago Baseball Facility from Phoenix Muni, travel north on Priest Drive until it becomes Galvin Parkway, which itself turns into 64th Street. Shortly thereafter the complex will be visible. It's just past the Scottsdale welcome sign.

SEATING
Phoenix Municipal Stadium has a capacity of 8,500. That makes it the smallest ballpark in the Cactus League, which has 10 ballparks with an average capacity of 10,897. As for where the A's play, all seats in their stadium have backs. Traditional chair back seats with cup holders are between the dugouts, while bleacher-style benches are beyond. Phoenix Muni has no berm, making it the only Cactus League ballpark that's sans the green stuff in the outfield.

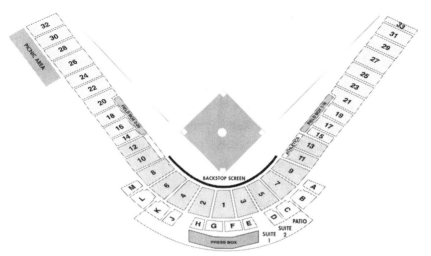

Phoenix Municipal Stadium Seating Chart

SECTIONS & TICKET PRICES

Field Box
Sections 2-20
Two rows of folding chairs that are in front of outfield reserved (bleacher) sections 14-21.
 Cost: $25

Lower Box
Sections 1-13
Seat rows: 1 to 18 in section 1; 1 to 15 in sections 2-3; 1 to 18 in sections 4-7; 2 to 15 in sections 8-9; 3 to 15 in sections 10-13
A better buy than the less comfortable and more distant Field Box seats, the 13 sections of Lower Box seats span from dugout to dugout and feature traditional stadium seating that is painted dark green.
 Cost: $22

Upper Box
Sections A-H and J-M
Seat rows: 1 to 11 in sections A-C; 1 to 7 in sections D-H and J; 1 to 11 in sections K-M
These are the best seats in the house for two reasons. First, most are covered by a concrete roof that shades them from the omnipresent sun. Secondly, the Upper Box seats are elevated enough that they allow for wonderful views of the stadium's impressive backdrop. As a bonus, the views of the playing field are great too. All 12 sections contain the same style of seating found in the Lower Box sections.
Cost: $18

Outfield Reserved
Sections 14-33
Seat rows: 5 to 18 in sections 14-19; 1 to 18 in sections 20-33
The cheap seats, of which there are plenty, are bleachers with backs. They begin just beyond the dugouts and extend down the outfield lines to the foul poles.
Cost: $12

Handicapped Seating
Handicap accessible seating is available in railed off platforms at the top of sections 2, 3, 8-13. If needed, additional space for wheelchairs is found on the concourse directly behind sections 16-21.

VIP seating
Two suites (each has 16 seats but can hold up to 22 people) and an open-air patio plaza (50 person capacity) are next to the press box on the stadium's first base side.

The red rock buttes of neighboring Papago Park provide a stunning backdrop for fans sitting on the first base side of the ballpark.

WHAT YOU NEED TO KNOW BEFORE YOU GO

1. The A's dugout is on the first base side. To make sure you're on the home side of the stadium, buy your tickets in sections A-F or in any odd numbered section.

2. An aisle divides the seating in the main grandstand into two sections. Lower Box seats are below the aisle and Upper Box seats are above it.

3. The protective screen behind home plate extends from sections 1-7 but is barely noticeable to those sitting behind it.

4. To enjoy views of Papago Park from your seat, you definitely want to sit on the first base side of the stadium. Fans on the third base side will be treated to a continual procession of planes descending to land at nearby Phoenix Sky Harbor airport.

5. Standing room is plentiful on the wide concourses behind the bleacher (Outfield Reserved) sections.

6. If the stands aren't full the ushers aren't restrictive when it comes to moving about the ballpark.

Seats to avoid
Steel light towers rising from within the grandstand obstruct the views of these Outfield Reserved bleacher seats:
- In section 20: seats 5-16 in rows 16-18
- In section 21: seats 1-10 in row 16 and seats 1-12 in rows 17-18
- In section 22: seats 1-4 in row 17 and seats 1-6 in row 18
- In section 23: seats 10-11 in row 17 and seats 7-12 in row 18

Seats in the shade
The stadium's roof covers rows 3 & up in all Upper Box sections (A-M). All rows in those same sections are in the shade shortly after the game starts (by 1:30). Shade continues to creep downward during the game as the sun descends behind the grandstand and by 2:30 fans in rows 12 & up in sections 1, 3, 5, 7 (first base side) enjoy freedom from the Arizona sun.

BUYING TICKETS
There are three ways to purchase tickets for A's games at Phoenix Municipal Stadium:
1. Online at www.oaklandathletics.com.
2. By calling **1-877-493-2255**.
3. In person. Beginning February 7, the stadium's box office is open from 10 a.m. to 4 p.m. on Monday through Friday and 10 a.m. to 2 p.m. on Saturday.

Children
Prior to their 2nd birthday, kids get in free and do not need a ticket.

GAME DAY
Gates open early at Phoenix Muni - 11:05 a.m. for the usual 1:05 p.m. start. But by then the A's have just finished batting practice

and without a lot of distractions in the stadium it's ill advised to get there so early, especially since the visiting team usually takes BP before they make the trip into Phoenix.

Food, drink and bag policy
- Bottles of water are allowed to be brought in, cans of anything are not.
- Bags up to a maximum size of 16" x 16" x 8" are permitted.

Getting autographs
The best place to get autographs is behind the bullpens, which are down the foul lines. Only about two feet separates fans from the benches pitchers sit on. A's fans should station themselves in sections 27 or 29, while visiting team fans should be in sections 26 or 28. Not only are those great places for autographs, but you can also hear conversations between players and coaches during pre-game bullpen sessions. It's one of the more intimate aspects of spring training.

The normal place fans congregate for autographs is no good here, as the dugout areas provide poor access. The tunnels that lead to each team's clubhouse are at the far end of their respective dugouts, but those walkways are covered by a tarp that effectively blocks fans out.

True autograph hounds should take note that the visiting team bus is parked next to the left field entry gate. Stick around about 20 minutes after the game and players will begin to emerge from their clubhouse to board the bus, which has only a small barricade set up in front of it. Many players, all in their street clothes by then, will come over and sign for those who wait around.

The bullpens are the place to be for a bevy of pre-game autographs.

FOOD FOR THOUGHT

Your taste buds will scorn the lack of creativity here. The menu is almost exclusively standard stuff (hot dogs, nachos, peanuts, etc.) For something different, visit one of the concession stands found on the elevated grassy picnic areas in both outfield corners. Portabella mushroom burgers are featured in left field.

SODA AND SUDS

The food may be pedestrian but you'll find a decent selection of beer on tap. Included in the mix in the past has been Blue Moon and Pyramid Hefeweizen. The non-alcohol selection is pretty good, with Arizona Tea, Gatorade and Pepsi leading the way.

AREA INFO

An outdoor lover's paradise is quite literally across the street from Phoenix Muni. That's where the southern edge of 1,200-acre Papago Park begins. The park is well-known for its geologic formations, the most famous of which is the appropriately

The A's will play 16 games in 2011 at Phoenix Muni, where they went 6-6-3 in 2010 before an average crowd of 5,966.

named Hole-in-the-Rock. In addition to other red rock formations, the park is home to the Phoenix Zoo, Desert Botanical Gardens, Municipal Golf Course, hiking and biking trails, and Hunt's Tomb, the white pyramid burial place of Arizona's first governor. For those who prefer a different type of post-game activity, the Valley's top party area is a few minutes' drive to the south, where bars and other nightlife hotspots reside on Tempe's Mill Avenue. Basically, there's a little bit of everything nearby.

Travelers' notes
- The closest Interstate, I-10, is about 2 miles away.
- Phoenix Sky Harbor International Airport is 4.7 miles away.
- The stadium is just 3 miles from Arizona State's campus in Tempe.
- The surrounding area is completely safe as it's at the southern edge of one of Phoenix's most popular tourist destinations.

NEARBY HOTELS
Approximate distance (in miles) to the ballpark is listed in parenthesis.

Motel 6 (0.6)
5315 E Van Buren St
Phoenix, AZ 85008
Phone: 602-267-8555

Hyatt Place (1.3)
1413 W Rio Salado Pkwy
Tempe, AZ 85281
Phone: 480-804-9544

SpringHill Suites (1.3)
1601 W Rio Salado Pkwy
Tempe, AZ 85281
Phone: 480-968-8222

Radisson (1.8)
427 N 44th St
Phoenix, AZ 85008
Phone: 602-220-4400

NEARBY RESTAURANTS
Approximate distance (in miles) to the ballpark is listed in parenthesis.

Ladybug Cafe (0.3)
1295 W Washington St
Tempe, AZ 85281
Phone: 602-681-9111

Port of Subs (0.5)
1158 W Washington St
Tempe, AZ 85281
Phone: 602-220-0775

Hap's Pit Barbecue (0.85)
4801 E Washington St
Phoenix, AZ 85034
Phone: 602-267-0181

Stockyards Restaurant (0.95)
5009 E Washington St
Phoenix, AZ 85034
Phone: 602-273-7378

LOOKING BACK AT LAST YEAR
The A's had an average spring at Phoenix Muni, where they won as often as they lost and managed to have three tie games. The team averaged 5,966 per home game, which ranked the A's 9th out of the 15 teams that trained in Arizona in 2010.

2010 Home Record: 6-6-3
Highest Attendance: 9,038 (vs. Diamondbacks on March 18)
Lowest Attendance: 2,488 (vs. Rangers on March 9)

2011 A'S HOME SCHEDULE

SUN	MON	TUES	WED	THURS	FRI	SAT
		1 Reds	2 Indians	3	4 Rangers	5 Giants
6 Brewers	7 Mariners	8 Padres	9	10 Royals	11 Dodgers	12
13 Rockies	14	15 Cubs	16	17 Cubs	18	19 White Sox
20 D-backs	21	22	23	24	25 Angels	26 Rockies
27	28	29	30	31		

The game on March 26 starts at 7:05 p.m.
All other games start at 1:05 p.m. local time.
For the full A's spring training schedule, see page 175.

SALT RIVER FIELDS
7555 North Pima Road
Scottsdale, AZ 85258

The 2011 season represents the end of one spring training era and the beginning of another for the Diamondbacks and Rockies, who left their separate homes in Tucson to join the rest of the Cactus League's teams in the metro Phoenix area, where the D-backs and Rox have joined forces to inhabit the fifth actively shared spring training complex in Arizona. The teams' move to the Valley of the Sun from The Old Pueblo officially ended Tucson's 64-season run as a training site for Major League teams. Tucson was the only winter home that the Diamondbacks and Rockies had ever known and was also, at one time, host to the Indians and White Sox.

LOCATION
The Cactus League's newest spring training stadium is at the center of a 140-acre complex built on land belonging to the Salt River Pima-Maricopa Indian Community (SRPMIC) that was previously home to an 18-hole golf course. Although it has a Scottsdale address, the stadium is just barely east of that city's limits. It is visible from the Loop 101 freeway, which marks the eastern boundary of the complex.

DIRECTIONS
Take Loop 101 (aka Pima Freeway) to the Indian Bend Road exit (#44) and go west until you come to Pima Road. Turn right (north) on Pima and the stadium is about a half-mile away on the right. Alternatively, the stadium can also be reached from the 101 by exiting at Via de Ventura Road (exit #43) and traveling west to Pima Road, onto which a left turn is made. Then the stadium is a short distance ahead on the left.

PARKING
Lots scattered about the complex collectively hold an estimated 3,000 cars.
 Cost: $5

BALLPARK BASICS
Capacity: 11,000
Opened: 2011
Construction cost: $100 million
Primary architect: HKS Architects

Owned and operated by the Salt River Pima-Maricopa Indian Community.

Outfield Dimensions   Phone:
LF: 345' CF: 410' RF: 345'   480-270-5000

BALLPARK OVERVIEW
Salt River Fields is modeled after Camelback Ranch. Each were designed by HKS Architects and built by Mortenson Construction. Similarities include the price tag of the entire complex ($100 million) and a lake stocked with fish leading up

to the stadium's main entrance. The two complexes are almost identical in size (Glendale's, at 141 acres, is an acre bigger) and each has walking trails from its parking lots that were designed to give fans intimate access to the dozen full-sized practice fields through which they weave. Fortunately for fans visiting Salt River Fields shade will be plentiful in the grandstand, where it's mostly absent in Camelback Ranch, thanks to a uniquely designed roof that mimics the traditional Native American ramada. Such a touch is important to the group that funded the entire cost of the complex, the Salt River Pima-Maricopa Indian Community. The motto for the facility they own is "Two Tribes. Two Teams. One Home." The Pima and Maricopa tribes joined forces in 1879 and 130 years later they were able to lure the Diamondbacks and Rockies away from Tucson and to their reservation by agreeing to build the teams a home that they officially named Salt River Fields at Talking Stick on June 4, 2010. The name was chosen to pay homage to the tribes' heritage and to further their "Talking Stick" brand, which was first applied to a nearby golf course and casino.

Outside the Park

The stadium's main entrance is behind home plate, where a cactus and tree landscaped plaza is reached via a bridge that spans a manmade water feature. Additional gates have been placed in the left and right field corners and center field. The center field gate will actually be the most used, as it's positioned near the parking lot where most fans will park.

The three-acre lake at the complex was stocked with 17,330 fish in June of 2010. The fish will be able to control algae and insects so that chemicals won't have to be used in the lake, which is used to irrigate everything green within the 140-acre complex.

Inside the Park

The concourse completely circles the playing field and will often be open on both sides, as the stadium will not have a traditional facade to serve as the concourse's back wall. Such a design is similar to the Brewers' Maryvale Baseball Park.

The bullpens are in the outfield corners instead of being cut into the berm. Each bullpen will begin at the end of the grandstand, the D-backs down the left field line and the Rockies in right.

The main scoreboard is in left-center field at the top of the berm and is a whopper. Measuring 48' wide by 24' high it's the largest in the Cactus League and is state-of-the-art all the way as the whole screen can display LED video.

A kids' area was placed in right field. The highlight there for the young'uns will likely be the wiffle ball field that is sponsored by Cold Stone Creamery, hence the name Cold Stone Kids Fun Field.

PRACTICE FIELDS

Each team has use of six full-sized practice fields, two half fields for infield practice, and 10 covered batting cages. Some of the practice areas are open to the public at all times. Fans wanting to watch February practice sessions will have access to all (or most) of the complex starting at 9 a.m.

SEATING

As is custom in new ballparks, all seats are of the chair back variety with armrests and cup holders. The berm spans the length of the outfield, broken up only by the sizable building behind the batter's eye in straight-away center field.

Salt River Fields Seating Chart

SECTIONS & TICKET PRICES

Infield Box
Sections 109-115
Found between the dugouts and centered behind home plate, these seven sections are considered to have the best seats in the house, if you go by price alone.
 Cost: $25

Dugout Reserve
Sections 104-108 and 116-120
The majority of the seats in these 10 sections are, as their name suggests, behind the dugouts. The exceptions are found in sections 104 and 120, which are next to a dugout. These seats are as close as you can get to the infield without having to peer through any type of netting, like the kind traditionally found behind home plate.
  Cost: $21

Infield Reserve
Sections 203-221
Easily the largest type of seating within the grandstand, the Infield Reserve sections offer something very much in demand at any Arizona-based ballpark during the afternoon: shade. The roof above these 19 sections ensures their popularity, as most of the 16 rows in each section are covered by it. All but the end sections (203-04 and 220-21) are within the infield.
  Cost: $20

Baseline Reserve
Sections 101-103 and 121-123
Found at field level down the outfield lines, these are the sunniest seats you can buy.
  Cost: $15

Lawn
General Admission
The berm is capable of holding 4,000 people, making it the largest found in a spring training ballpark.
  Cost: $8

Handicapped Seating

Handicap accessible seating is found at the top of sections 103-104, 109, 115, 120-121, 206-208, 210-214, and 216-218.

VIP seating

At press box/suite level, open-air party decks are even with first and third base. Each is sponsored by a brand of reduced-alcohol beer (Coors Light and Miller Lite) and can hold 200 people. Behind home plate and atop the press box is the Pepsi Patio, a supersized party deck that will give up to 400 people breathtaking views of the complex and its mountainous backdrop. The ticket price for all three party decks is $19 per person. Pepsi Patio tickets are sold to anybody who wants them while tickets in the Coors Light Cold Zone and Miller Lite Taste Zone are offered to groups first, then as single game tickets if they are still available on (or close to) game day. For those wanting something more upscale than a party deck, the stadium has four 15-person capacity luxury suites.

WHAT YOU NEED TO KNOW BEFORE YOU GO

1. The Diamondbacks dugout is on the third base side. To make sure you're on the Arizona side of the stadium, buy your tickets in sections 113-123 or 213-221.
2. The Rockies dugout is on the first base side. To make sure you're on the Colorado side of the stadium, buy your tickets in sections 101-112 or 203-212.
3. There are 28 rows of seating within the grandstand and an aisle divides them unequally. The 16 rows above the aisle are mostly under the stadium's roof and thereby shaded. Closer to the field and below the aisle are 12 rows and the top two-thirds of them will be in the shade by early afternoon.
4. Fans will enjoy views of various mountain ranges, most notably Camelback Mountain and the McDowell Mountains.

As this architectural rendering shows, the roof, which has two panels that overlap behind home plate, is positioned so that most seats in the grandstand will be shaded during the course of the afternoon.

Seats in the shade

According to a press release on studies done by the architects, virtually all fans attending spring training games in March that sit above the cross aisle (i.e. in the Infield Reserve seats) will be in the shade for the entire game while approximately 85 percent of the fans in the 7,000 fixed seats will be shaded as the game progresses.

BUYING TICKETS

There are three ways to purchase tickets for games at Salt River Fields:

1. Online at www.ticketmaster.com, www.dbacks.com/spring or www.coloradorockies.com/spring.

2. By calling **888-490-0383** or **480-362-9467**.

3. In person, either at the temporary ticket office in the Scottsdale Pavilions (8980 E. Indian Bend Road, Suite D-6) or at the stadium box office when it's completed. Prior to games beginning, hours of operation at either option are 10 a.m. to 6 p.m. on Monday through Friday and 10 a.m. to 4 p.m. on

Saturday. When the season has begun, the temporary location will be closed and the stadium's box office will have daily hours of 9 a.m. to 5 p.m. Additionally, tickets can be bought at the Chase Field box office.

Children
Ages 2 & under who are sitting on the lap of an adult do not need a game ticket.

GAME DAY
The center field gate is the first to open, which it does 2 hours and 40 minutes prior to game time. So fans can enter the ballpark as early as 10:30 a.m. for an afternoon game and 4:00 p.m. for an evening game. The ballpark's other three gates open 2 hours and 10 minutes prior to game time, which translates into 11:00 a.m. or 4:30 p.m. for a day or night game.

Food, drink and bag policy
- A single factory-sealed bottle of water, up to one liter in size, per fan is allowed to be brought inside.
- No food can be brought inside the stadium.
- Soft-sided bags and containers up to a maximum size of 16" x 16" x 8" are permitted.

Getting autographs
The official company line from the folks at Salt River Fields is: "Guests are permitted to seek autographs from players along the railing between sections 101-104 and 120-123 up to 40 minutes prior to game time, or until the end of batting practice, whichever comes first." Also, according to *The Arizona Republic*, "the Diamondbacks intend to have a designated spot in left field near the clubhouse where players can meet with fans and sign

autographs." There's no word at press time on whether the Rockies have similar intentions.

FOOD FOR THOUGHT

Local restaurants that have signed on to sell their goods at concession stands include Crust Gourmet Pizza Bar, Native New Yorker and Salty Senorita. The headquarters for Cold Stone Creamery are close to the stadium and the national chain's ice cream will be served there. Vegetarians will find more options than normal, as specialty wraps, salads, bean burritos and sweet potato fries are part of the healthy selections line-up. In all, the stadium has eight permanent concession stands and over 25 portable carts will be set up on game day.

AREA INFO

Although Salt River Fields at Talking Stick is built on an Indian reservation, that reservation has been developed commercially by the Salt River Pima-Maricopa Indian Community to become an entertainment destination, and as thus is anything but remote. Close to the stadium, the tribes' 15-story, 497-room Talking Stick Resort opened in 2010 adjacent to their always open Casino Arizona, which has 240,000 square feet of gambling space. Near the casino and resort is the Talking Stick Golf Club, a 36-hole public course that was designed by Ben Crenshaw's firm and opened in 1997. While much development has yet to take place, Scottsdale Pavilions has been open for two decades and contains numerous specialty stores, national retailers and restaurants on both sides of Indian Bend Road, which is the road most fans will arrive at the spring training complex by.

Travelers' notes

- The closest major highway is the Loop 101, which runs alongside the facility.
- Phoenix Sky Harbor International Airport is 17.1 miles away.
- The stadium is 22 miles northeast of the Diamondbacks' regular season home, Chase Field, which is in downtown Phoenix.

NEARBY HOTELS

Approximate distance (in miles) to the ballpark is listed in parenthesis.

The Inn at Pima (0.1)
7330 N Pima Rd
Scottsdale, AZ 85260
Phone: 480-948-3800

Country Inn & Suites (2.9)
10801 N 89th Place
Scottsdale, AZ 85260
Phone: 480-314-1200

Hampton Inn (3.6)
10101 N Scottsdale Rd
Scottsdale, AZ 85253
Phone: 480-443-3233

NEARBY RESTAURANTS

Approximate distance (in miles) to the ballpark is listed in parenthesis.

Sweet Tomatoes (0.75)
9029 E Indian Bend Rd
Scottsdale, AZ 85250
Phone: 480-991-6010

Five & Diner (0.8)
9069 E Indian Bend Rd
Scottsdale, AZ 85250
Phone: 480-949-1957

YC's Mongolian Grill (0.85)
9120 E Indian Bend Rd
Scottsdale, AZ 85250
Phone: 480-948-8011

Denny's (0.9)
9160 E Indian Bend Rd
Scottsdale, AZ 85250
Phone: 480-991-2909

This is what the site of Salt River Fields looked like on March 31, 2010, which was the day the Diamondbacks and Rockies played their final spring training game in Tucson.

LOOKING BACK AT LAST YEAR

The Diamondbacks and Rockies finished their tenures as Tucson-based teams with winning home records although Arizona, as they always did, easily outdrew Colorado in drawing fans to the ballpark. The D-back's 6,647 per game home average placed them 6th in the Cactus League. The Rockies' average crowd of 5,243 at venerable Hi Corbett Field was good for just 13th place, ahead of only the two teams training in Goodyear.

2010 Diamondbacks Home Record: 8-7
Highest Attendance: 11,571 (vs. Dodgers on March 13)
Lowest Attendance: 3,141 (vs. Indians on March 8)

2010 Rockies Home Record: 10-5
Highest Attendance: 7,273 (vs. Cubs on March 15)
Lowest Attendance: 2,337 (vs. Diamondbacks on March 7)

2011 DIAMONDBACKS HOME SCHEDULE

SUN	MON	TUES	WED	THURS	FRI	SAT
						26 Rockies
27 Giants	28 Rockies	1	2 Mariners	3	4 Padres	5 Rangers
6	7	8	9 Brewers	10 White Sox	11	12
13 Cubs	14	15 Giants	16 Angels	17	18	19 Reds
20	21 Dodgers	22 Indians	23	24 A's	25	26 Royals
27	28 Rangers	29	30	31		

The games on March 10, 15 & 21 start at 6:40 p.m.

All other games start at 1:10 p.m. local time.

For the full Diamondbacks spring training schedule, see page 165.

2011 ROCKIES HOME SCHEDULE

SUN	MON	TUES	WED	THURS	FRI	SAT
27	28	1 D-backs	2	3 Giants	4	5
6 Indians	7 Dodgers	8 Cubs	9	10	11 Royals	12 Padres D-backs
13	14 Reds	15	16	17 White Sox	18 Brewers	19
20 Angels	21	22	23 Mariners	24	25 Rangers	26
27 A's	28	29 Mariners	30	31		

The games on March 12 (2nd game), 23 & 25 start at 6:40 p.m.

All other games start at 1:10 p.m. local time.

For the full Rockies spring training schedule, see page 170.

SCOTTSDALE STADIUM

7408 East Osborn Road
Scottsdale, AZ 85251

The 2011 season will be the 31st that the Giants have trained in Scottsdale and 64th overall in Arizona. No other franchise has spent more years training in the Grand Canyon State and only the Cubs (by two years) have been in their present host city longer.

LOCATION

Scottsdale Stadium takes up 11 acres in the heart of the city's downtown and can rightfully make the claim as spring training's most urban ballpark. It stands on a busy city thoroughfare just three blocks from Old Town Scottsdale and directly across the street from the Scottsdale Healthcare Hospital.

DIRECTIONS

From Loop 101:
Exit at Indian School Road (exit #47). Go west for roughly 1.7 miles on Indian School, then south on Drinkwater Boulevard. The stadium is at the intersections of Drinkwater and Osborn Road.

From Loop 202:
Exit at Scottsdale Road (exit #7) and travel north approximately 3.3 miles. Bear right onto Drinkwater Boulevard and the stadium will be a half-mile ahead on your right.

PARKING

The one true negative to Scottsdale Stadium's highly visible downtown location is parking. There is a small paved lot on the stadium's first base side, but it's not available on game day to the public. Many of the seemingly available spaces near the ballpark are actually reserved for hospital parking. An exception is the free public parking garage directly behind left field on Drinkwater Boulevard, but it fills up well before game time. Another good option is the Parking Corral, found in the heart of Old Town at the intersections of E 2nd Street and Brown Avenue. It's a free deck just a few blocks from Drinkwater and one past the Scottsdale Museum of Contemporary Art. More parking is scattered throughout downtown. The later you arrive the further away you will park. One way to avoid the hassle is to opt for the Giants' Trolley Shuttle. The free service begins 90 minutes before game time and concludes 30 minutes after the last pitch. A map of park and ride stops is available online at www.scottsdaletrolley.com. Full details on the shuttle can be heard by calling 480-421-1004.

Cost: Varies, from free to fee

BALLPARK BASICS
Capacity: 12,000
Opened: 1992
Construction cost: $8.4 million
Primary architect: HOK Sport

Owned by the city of Scottsdale and operated by the Scottsdale Charros.

First game: The Giants defeated the Mariners 2-1 on March 12, 1992 in front of 7,742 fans.

Outfield Dimensions
LF: 360' CF: 430' RF: 360'

Phone:
480-990-7972

BALLPARK OVERVIEW

The playing field at Scottsdale Stadium has resided on the same spot since 1955. But the stadium surrounding the field was gutted, rebuilt and reopened in 1992 thanks to the generosity of Scottsdale taxpayers, who approved the largest bond issue in city history to make sure the Giants, and spring training, remained in their city. The public's money was well spent as HOK Sport designed a gorgeous structure, highlighted by red brick and dark green wrought iron. Inside and out, the stadium is immaculately manicured. Over 200 trees provide a pleasing backdrop. Impressive views of the surrounding Camelback mountain ranges make a favorable lasting impression from most grandstand seats, especially on the first base side. Perhaps the only drawback to the stadium is its overabundance of aluminum. Half of the upper grandstand is filled with it, in the form of bleacher-style benches, and bleacher seats outnumber traditional plastic chairs. Other than that, Scottsdale Stadium is the perfect place to watch a ballgame.

Outside the Park

Fans have the choice of entering the ballpark through one of six gates surrounding it. Gate A is behind center field, Gate B is behind first base, Gates C & D are behind home plate, Gate E is behind third base and serves as the stadium's main entrance, and Gate F is in left field, where it serves as the main lawn seating entrance.

Gate A is next to a col-de-sac that serves as a non-congested drop-off point for groups and other individuals.

Ticket windows are adjacent to Gates B and E. The ticket windows next to gate F are primarily for lawn seating.

Will Call is located at the Gate B box office only.

Inside the Park

The concourse is located behind the stadium and is partly covered by the grandstand. It's also home to the Arizona Fall League Hall of Fame and Scottsdale Sports Hall of Fame. Plaques for inductees of both are on the concourse's wall behind home plate.

The Giants' bullpen is in right field, behind the fence and below the Charro Lodge. The visitors' bullpen is behind the left field fence, adjacent to the foul pole.

The stadium's main scoreboard is behind the berm in left-center field. It has a video board, electronic line score, and is topped by a hand dial clock. A small scoreboard is attached to the façade of both the first and third base grandstand.

Camelback Mountain provides a scenic backdrop for fans sitting on the first base side of Scottsdale Stadium, while over 200 trees surround the grounds of the stadium that's found in the heart of downtown.

Fans are never far from a souvenir shop. The ballpark has six, including the main team store behind first base (near Gate B).

PRACTICE FIELDS

The Giants' practice field is directly behind right field. They use it and the Scottsdale Stadium field for all of their workouts. The stadium's gates open around 10 a.m. for fans wanting to watch February practice sessions. Workouts on the adjacent practice field can be watched from the stadium's concourse in the right field corner, which is elevated so you can see into that field just fine. Granted, that's not the best set-up or the norm, as at most complexes you can stand right behind home plate, or at least close to it, and at field level.

The team's four-field minor league training facility is 1.8 miles away in Indian School Park, which is located at 4415 North Hayden Road. To get to the Giants' minor league complex from Scottsdale Stadium, take East Osborn Road to North Hayden Road and drive until it intersects Camelback Road. One issue that might want to make you avoid the trip to minor league camp is that all of the fences there are windscreened, so visibility is extremely limited.

115

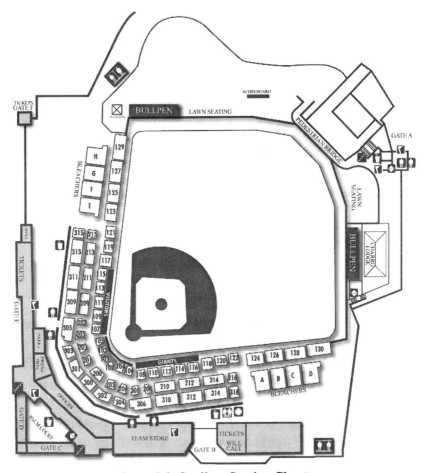

Scottsdale Stadium Seating Chart

SEATING

Scottsdale Stadium has a larger than league average capacity of 12,000 and the Giants have historically been the Cactus League's second best draw, trailing only the Cubs in average home attendance. Bleacher seats outnumber stadium seats by a 4,500 to 3,688 count. The embankment used for lawn seating has a capacity of 3,812.

SECTIONS & TICKET PRICES

* Ticket prices vary as the Giants use dynamic pricing, which means prices will fluctuate depending on a number of factors. Because of this, each seating section has a price range, rather than a set price.

Lower Box

Sections 101-122

Seat rows: D to F in sections 101-102; A to F in sections 103-106; C to H in sections 107-116; A to H in sections 117-118; A to F in sections 119-122

As their name suggests, the Lower Box seats make up the lower portion of seating in the main grandstand and they wrap all the way around the infield, beginning and ending just past the infield dirt. These seats put you closest to the playing field but many of them are pre-sold to season tickets holders, which limits their availability to the general public.

Cost: $26 to $35

Upper Box

Sections 200-216

Seat rows: J to O in all sections

The first six rows of seats above the grandstand's interior cross-aisle are the only "upper" sections to have stadium seating instead of bleachers. Like their Lower Box counterparts, the Upper Box seats are limited in availability on a game-by-game basis as many of them are gobbled up by season ticket holders.

Cost: $22 to $32

Reserved Grandstand

300-306 and 309-316

Seat rows: 1 to 6 in sections 300-304 and 306; 1 to 8 in sections 305 and 309-316

These are the best bleachers seats you can buy at a Cactus League ballpark. They begin immediately after row O of Upper

Box seating. Many of them are shaded and all have seats backs. The Reserved Grandstand's bleachers are unique since they are the only ones surrounding the infield at one of the league's 11 ballparks.
 Cost: $20 to $31

Line Box

Sections 123-126
Seat rows: A to H in all sections
These are four field level sections that reside down the outfield line and just beyond the seating bowl that makes up the main grandstand. The seats are not angled towards home plate, so craning your neck in that direction is necessary.
 Cost: $19 to $29

Outfield Box

Sections 127-130
Seat rows: A to H in sections 127-128; A to F in section 129; A to G in section 130
The only real reason to sit here is if you want a fixed seat and all the other non-bleachers are sold out. The stadium seating in the four Outfield Box sections is at field level but so far down each respective outfield line that fans sitting in them are a good ways away from home plate, which the seats are not angled towards.
 Cost: $16 to $25

Bleachers

Sections A-H
Seat rows: 1 to 15 in all sections
In a stadium full of aluminum benches these are the least fancy as they don't have seat backs. Just like the Line and Outfield Box seats below them, the Bleachers are facing the outfield instead of the diamond.
 Cost: $13 to $24

Although shaded seats are in short supply within Scottsdale Stadium, select fans in the left field berm are able to enjoy tree provided cover.

Lawn
General Admission
Extending from left field to right-center, the Scottsdale Stadium berm is very popular among 20-somethings. It's festive, beautifully landscaped and mostly definitely "the place to be," making the berm in Scottsdale the best of its kind in the Cactus League.
 Cost: $9 to $21

Handicapped Seating
Handicap accessible seating is available on platforms at the top of sections 101-106, 119-122, and 129-130.

VIP seating
The split-level Charro Lodge in right field has a covered pavilion and large terrace patio. It's named after and operated

119

by the Scottsdale Charros, the local civic organization that has run spring training for the city since 1964. There's also a picnic terrace next to the press box that can be reserved by groups. A private picnic area that wraps around the left field foul pole is available to all fans on days it's not booked by groups.

WHAT YOU NEED TO KNOW BEFORE YOU GO

1. The Giants dugout is on the first base side. To make sure you're on the home side of the stadium, buy your tickets in any even numbered section.
2. An aisle cuts through the middle of the grandstand. Lower, Line, and Outfield Box seats are below the cross-aisle, while Upper Box, Reserved Grandstand and Bleachers are above it.
3. Seats do not have cup holders.
4. The protective screen behind home plate is small, in no way impedes views, and doesn't prevent foul pop-ups from landing in the sections (101-106) behind it.
5. The berm is unusual in that its concourse runs behind the left field portion, completely obstructed from the playing field, before it rises on the right field side, where it's above and open to the playing field.
6. Standing room is limited to the crest of the berm in left, the concourse behind it in right-center, and a small grassy area between the right field foul pole and Charro Lodge.
7. Ushers will let you move freely about the ballpark and upgrade your seat if better ones are available, which isn't often the case as the stadium is filled to capacity for a majority of its games.

Seats to avoid

If you don't like bleachers, be forewarned there are plenty of them here and the freestanding sections (A-H) down each outfield line don't have seat backs. Also, the sections beyond the main grandstand (Line and Outfield Box plus Bleachers) have seats that are angled towards the outfield instead of the infield, which can be a slight nuisance that has been corrected in newer ballparks but still remains in the older ones, such as 19-year "old" Scottsdale Stadium.

Seats in the shade

Rows 3 & up in Reserved Grandstand sections 300-306 and 309-310 are covered by the press box's awning and by 2:30 all rows in those sections have shade cast upon them, as the sun descends behind the grandstand. Your only other option is the left field berm, where many a fan is shaded by trees. But in general, not much shade is found here.

BUYING TICKETS

There are three ways to purchase tickets for Giants games at Scottsdale Stadium:

1. Online at www.sfgiants.com.
2. By calling **1-877-473-4849**.
3. In person. The stadium's box office is open from 10 a.m. to 5 p.m. on Monday through Friday. Fans in the San Francisco area can purchase spring training tickets directly from the AT&T Park ticket office or at one of the Giants Dugout Stores.

Children

Ages 2 & under get in free and do not require a ticket.

GAME DAY

Gates open two hours prior to game time, which is earlier than most ballparks but still not early enough to watch the Giants take batting practice. And since most visiting teams take BP at their home ballpark before busing over to Scottsdale there's not much going on in the stadium until close to game time.

Food, drink and bag policy

- One sealed plastic bottle of water per person is allowed inside.
- Food cannot be brought into the stadium.
- Small bags and backpacks are permitted following an inspection.

Getting autographs

Within a half-hour of the game starting players from both teams begin to sign autographs next to their dugouts. Giants players frequent section 118 the most, while visiting players pick and choose spots down the left field line, especially the pitchers en route to their bullpen in left field.

Since the tunnels to the clubhouses for both teams are located in the dugouts players don't sign during games.

Post-game autographs are easiest to obtain from visiting pitchers, who once again have to walk close to the stands to get back to their dugout. The Giants' bullpen is in right-center, so their approach back to their dugout isn't as fan-friendly.

FOOD FOR THOUGHT

Vendors walk the concourse and sell beer from tubs filled with ice. Unfortunately, the only thing to go with the cold beer is a pedestrian selection of food, highlighted by barbeque. San Franciscans will recognize and appreciate the garlic fries from Gordon Biersch, while Dos Gringos occupies a noticeable snack and beverage stand atop the left-center field berm.

SODA AND SUDS

Beer on tap is plentiful, with different selections available at different concessions, ranging from microbrews to the big company breweries. In 2010, offerings found along the concourse ranged from San Fran's Anchor Steam to Milwaukee's Miller Lite. Fountain drinks are the domain of Coca-Cola.

AREA INFO

The city of Scottsdale refers to itself as "The West's Most Western Town" and Exhibit A of that moniker is Old Town Scottsdale, which is just a short walk away from the stadium. Shops, restaurants, arts and crafts can all be found in Old Town, which is designed to look like a classical western outpost. Barely outside of Old Town is Don and Charlie's, a restaurant definitely worth a visit if you like American food and America's pastime, as its walls are covered with a treasure trove of sports memorabilia, much of it baseball-related. As the stadium is located in a recently revitalized downtown, surrounding dining and destination options are plentiful and include the nearby Scottsdale Fashion Square, the largest shopping mall in the entire American Southwest. All in all, Scottsdale is tops in the Cactus League among cities to hang out in after the game.

Travelers' notes
- Two major highways are nearby - the Loop 101 and 202.
- Phoenix Sky Harbor International Airport is 7.4 miles away.
- The stadium is 5 miles from the Arizona State campus.
- All of Scottsdale is safe. The downtown stadium area is no exception.

Trivia Tidbit
Scottsdale Stadium hosted three games of the inaugural World Baseball Classic in 2006. All games involved South Africa, the final of which was played on March 10 against the United States. Team USA won that game 17-0.

NEARBY HOTELS
Approximate distance (in miles) to the ballpark is listed in parenthesis.

Comfort Suites (0.1)
3275 N Drinkwater Blvd
Scottsdale, AZ 85251
Phone: 480-946-1111

Courtyard Old Town (0.3)
3311 N Scottsdale Rd
Scottsdale, AZ 85251
Phone: 480-429-7785

Holiday Inn Express (0.35)
3131 N Scottsdale Rd
Scottsdale, AZ 85251
Phone: 480-675-7665

Homestead Suites (0.4)
3560 N Marshall Way
Scottsdale, AZ 85251
Phone: 480-994-0297

NEARBY RESTAURANTS
Approximate distance (in miles) to the ballpark is listed in parenthesis.

Olive Garden (0.25)
3380 N Scottsdale Rd
Scottsdale, AZ 85251
Phone: 480-874-0212

Red Lobster (0.25)
3360 N Scottsdale Rd
Scottsdale, AZ 85251
Phone: 480-675-9733

Blue Moose Sports Bar (0.3)
7373 E Scottsdale Mall
Scottsdale, AZ 85251
Phone: 480-949-7959

Tokyo Express (0.35)
3530 N Goldwater Blvd
Scottsdale, AZ 85251
Phone: 480-949-1004

The Giants will play 17 games in 2011 at Scottsdale Stadium, where they went 10-5 in 2010 before an average crowd of 10,388.

LOOKING BACK AT LAST YEAR

The Giants got off to a great start in the spring, going 21-10 in Arizona, and their winning ways continued all the way into November, culminating with their first world championship since moving to San Francisco in 1958. Their games in Scottsdale were very well attended -- six times they played to Scottsdale Stadium capacity -- and in all 155,819 filed through the turnstiles there, topping the Cactus League by 3,326 total fans over the Cubs, who played one less home game in Mesa. Because of that, the Cubs lead the 15-team league in average home game attendance. The Giants' average of 10,388 ranked them a solid second.

2010 Home Record: 10-5
Highest Attendance: 12,087 (vs. Angels on March 26)
Lowest Attendance: 5,547 (vs. White Sox on March 9)

2011 GIANTS HOME SCHEDULE

SUN	MON	TUES	WED	THURS	FRI	SAT
					25 D-backs	26 Dodgers
27	28	1 Cubs	2 D-backs	3	4 Brewers	5
6 Mariners	7 Rangers	8	9 White Sox	10	11	12 Dodgers
13	14 Brewers	15	16	17 Angels	18 Dodgers	19 Royals
20 A's	21 Rockies	22	23	24 Indians	25	26 Reds

The games on March 2, 7, 17 & 24 start at 7:05 p.m.

The game on March 26 starts at 3:10 p.m.

All other games start at 1:05 p.m. local time.

For the full Giants spring training schedule, see page 177.

SURPRISE STADIUM
15960 North Bullard Avenue
Surprise, AZ   85374

The 2011 season will be the 9th that the Rangers and Royals have jointly trained in Surprise, a city of about 100,000 residents that's 25 miles northwest of Phoenix.

LOCATION
Surprise Stadium is the centerpiece of the city's Surprise Recreation Campus, a 132-acre complex that includes a little bit of everything. In addition to baseball practice facilities, the campus is home to the city's aquatic center, tennis complex, a regional library, community park, and art museum, all of which are across the street from the stadium's main entrance.

DIRECTIONS
Take I-10 to the Loop 101 North. Exit at Grand Avenue (exit #11) and head west. Drive for 6 miles on Grand (aka Hwy 60) and turn left onto busy Bell Road. Go 1½ miles and turn left onto Bullard Avenue. The stadium is a short distance ahead on the right. You'll see its light towers from Bell Road.

PARKING
There's a small paved lot behind left field and then a large grass field beyond that to handle most overflow, with the rest of the excess parking in the paved lot across the street at the Surprise Aquatic Center. Both lots are close to the stadium and have a price that can't be beat.
Cost: Free

BALLPARK BASICS
Capacity: 10,500
Opened: 2003
Construction cost: $48.3 million
Primary architect: HOK Sport

Owned by the City of Surprise and operated on game day by the Surprise Sundancers.

First spring training game: The Royals defeated the Rangers 6-3 on February 27, 2003 in front of 3,382 fans.

Outfield Dimensions	Phone:
LF: 350' CF: 400' RF: 350'	623-222-2000

BALLPARK OVERVIEW
Surprise Stadium exudes a wow factor, as everything was done first class. Built on the former site of a World War II pilot training field, the stadium is essentially split into two halves. Everything Royals - dugout, bullpen, clubhouse, logos, banners - is on the left (third base) half; the Rangers get the same treatment on the right (first base) side. The stadium was built by HOK Sport and they followed the recent trend of including a small second deck. Surprise's upper level overhangs the lower

seating bowl. Those sitting in the Lower Dugout seats benefit from that design with shade, thanks in part to the sun descending behind the grandstand during the afternoon. The only ribbon scoreboards found at a spring training ballpark adorn the two facades of the upper level. Games are played on Billy Parker Field, named in honor of the former Angels infielder and city's first Parks and Recreation Director. Parker died a month before the first Cactus League game was played in Surprise. The entire facility is sometimes referred to as the Surprise Recreation Campus as the stadium also contains the city's Community and Recreation Services Department building.

Outside the Park

The backside of the main scoreboard serves as the stadium's welcome billboard, positioned so that it is visible from anywhere in the main parking lot.

Fans enter the ballpark at street level through gates in the outfield. The main entrance is behind center field. Lesser used gates can be found in left and right field, each slightly to the foul side of the foul pole.

All nine ticket windows are located just to the right of the center field gates. The Will Call table is an equally short distance away to the left of those same gates.

Inside the Park

The main concourse completely encircles and is open to the playing field. It's above the lower level seating bowl and covered only where it runs beneath the upper level. The upper level concourse is covered by a roof and has TVs.

Both bullpens are cut into the outfield berm near the foul poles - the Royals in left, Rangers in right.

The stadium's main scoreboard is located behind the berm in left-center field and has a video board and electronic line score. It also displays the speed of each pitch. Two scoreboards on either side of the upper level's facade list basic game information for fans sitting in the berm.

An area for kids can be found on the first base concourse. It features a mini wiffle ball field and carousel, which is free to ride.

Rangers fans have an opportunity to watch their team's hitters hit in the covered batting cage building near the merry-go-round at the back of the first base concourse, where only chain link fencing separates spectators from superstars (and many lesser known guys taking some hacks). The Royals have a similar back of the concourse batting cage setup along the third base concourse, but fan accessibility is blocked by a food court.

Two souvenir shops, both called The Sport Shop, carry a small selection of Rangers and Royals gear. The shops are located behind home plate and center field.

PRACTICE FIELDS

The training complexes for both teams are behind the main ballpark. The Royals' six fields are behind the left side; the Rangers' six fields are behind the right side.

Although they are in different locations, the practice field gates for both teams open at 10:00 a.m. Spectator parking for the Royals' practice facilities is in the main stadium's parking lot. Fans wishing to view Rangers practices and pre-game preparations should park in the lot at the intersections of Parkview Place and Major League Boulevard.

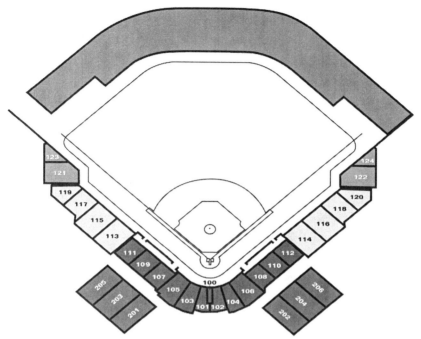

Surprise Stadium Seating Chart

SEATING

Surprise Stadium has a listed capacity of 10,500, a number that can be exceeded due to the copious amount of space for standing room on the concourse that compliments a berm that extends the entire length of the outfield. Surprise's stadium was the first in the Cactus League to be built without bleachers and the 7,000 seats in its grandstand all have cup holders in addition to the standard chair backs and armrests.

SECTIONS & TICKET PRICES

Lower Dugout
Sections 101-112
Seat rows: E to R in sections 101-102; B to V in sections 103-106;
D to T in sections 107-108; D to R in sections 109-110; D to T in
sections 111-112
A dozen sections of seating that extend from dugout to dugout,
Lower Dugout seats are generally shaded thanks to the second
level that's behind them. That makes what are already great
seats even better, and from here you'll enjoy great views of
everything but the local mountain ranges.
Cost: $24

Upper Dugout
Sections 201-206
Seat rows: A to G in all sections
Some of the best non-premium seats that fans at a Cactus
League ballpark can buy, there are three Upper Dugout sections
apiece on each side of the second-story press box. They
overhang the lower level, which puts them closer to the playing
field than normal upper level seats are, and that design makes
you feel like you're hovering above the playing field. Even
better, all seven rows in each of the six sections are covered by a
roof, so you'll have it made in the shade at a reasonable-by-
modern-day-standards price.
Cost: $21

Infield
Sections 113-120
Seat rows: A to V in sections 113-116; A to T in sections 117-118;
A to R in sections 119-120
Outfield Line Seats would be a more appropriate name, as that's
what the Infield Seats really are. Views from the four sections

(113-116) closer to the infield are much better than the four
sections (117-120) that are midway down each outfield line.
  Cost: $18

Plaza
Sections 121-124
Seat rows: A to V in sections 121-122; K to V in sections 123-124
The Plaza Seats make up the last two sections on each side of the
grandstand and are curved inward towards the playing field, a
design which makes them a better buy than the outermost half
of their Infield Seat counterparts. The Plaza Seats taper off at the
end of the grandstand, which doesn't quite extend to each foul
pole.
  Cost: $14

Lawn
General Admission
The berm can hold up to 3,600 people on its expanse of lush
grass that blankets the entire outfield, where the perfectly
sloped hill provides ideal views of the ballgame and ballpark.
  Cost: $7

Handicapped Seating
Handicap accessible seating is available in railed off platforms at
the top of sections 101-102, 107-112, 117-120 and 201-202.
Handicap seats are always in row V in the lower level and row
G in the upper level. In the outfield, a single row of unmarked
seating behind each bullpen is set aside as ADA seats.

VIP seating
Suites with outdoor balconies are on both sides of the press box
in the upper level. The Home Run Party Deck is in right field,
erected in the berm next to the Rangers bullpen. An all you can

eat buffet and drink voucher comes with the price ($30) of party deck admission.

WHAT YOU NEED TO KNOW BEFORE YOU GO

1. The Royals dugout is on the third base side. To make sure you're on the Kansas City side of the stadium, buy your tickets in any odd numbered section.
2. The Rangers dugout is on the first base side. To make sure you're on the Texas side of the stadium, buy your tickets in any even numbered section.
3. Rows I and O are skipped in all sections.
4. The protective screen behind the batter extends from sections 101-106 but is very unobtrusive, unlike some parks.
5. Most seats have at least a glimpse of the distant mountain ranges that ring the stadium. Fans in the right field berm and upper level have the best views of Arizona's natural skyline, which feature the Estrella and White Tank Mountains.
6. Standing room is plentiful on the 360-degree concourse, which includes numerous free standing tabletops and picnic tables for fans who don't want to eat in their seats.
7. Fans are free to roam the stadium and sit where they choose thanks to the friendly and lenient ushers, although the upper level is off-limits to non-ticket holders until after the 5th inning.

Seats to avoid

It's a minor detail, but seats in sections 117-120 are angled towards center field, not home plate.

Trivia Tidbit
The building of Surprise Stadium and its training facilities lured the Rangers and Royals to the Cactus League after the two franchises had spent their entire existences - a collective 76 spring trainings - in Florida's Grapefruit League.

Plenty of shade is provided by the stadium's small upper level, which overhangs some seats below it and blocks the sun's rays from reaching others in each of the dozen Lower Dugout sections.

Seats in the shade

The Upper Dugout seats (sections 201-206) are covered by a roof and they overhang sections 107-112, where rows N and up are covered by the overhang. Fans sitting in the Lower Dugout seats (sections 101-112) are protected from the sun thanks to the upper level, which blocks the rays completely at varying times depending on the section. By the time of a typical afternoon start (1:05), most seats in sections 101, 102, 104, 106, 108, 110 & 112 are in the shade and remain so throughout the game. Seats on the opposite side of the stadium (sections 103, 105, 107, 109 & 111) enjoy full shade by 2:30.

BUYING TICKETS

There are three ways to purchase tickets for games at Surprise Stadium:
1. Online at www.ticketmaster.com, www.royals.com or www.texasrangers.com.
2. By calling Ticketmaster at **800-745-3000**.
3. In person. The stadium's box office is open from 10 a.m. to 5 p.m. on Monday through Friday and from 10 a.m. to 2 p.m. on Saturday.

Children

Ages 2 & under are admitted free but are required to sit on a ticket holder's lap if in the grandstand.

GAME DAY

All gates open an hour and a half before game time.

Food, drink and bag policy

- One plastic bottle of water per fan is allowed inside, although the bottle must be sealed (unopened). Boxed fruit juices and baby formula are also permitted.
- Food can be brought into the stadium as long as it's presented in a clear, sealed plastic bag and is able to fit under a standard stadium seat.
- Bags can be brought inside provided they don't exceed the maximum allowable size of 16" x 16" x 8".

Getting autographs

Fans will have difficulty obtaining autographs before the game as teams generally don't take batting practice inside of Surprise Stadium. The Rangers and Royals instead hit on one of their practice fields while visiting teams often take BP in their home park before boarding their bus, which arrives in Surprise about an hour before game time. That's when fans of visiting teams should position themselves directly behind home plate and alongside the tunnel that is cut into sections 101 and 102. That tunnel is used by visiting players to get to and from their clubhouse and they have to utilize it to get to the playing field. Since the Rangers' and Royals' clubhouses are in the outfield corners their players don't have to come in close contact with fans unless they choose to. The good news is that when it gets closer to game time a handful of players will sign near their respective dugouts. The best place to station yourself is in

Nine Cactus League ballparks have a berm and only two of them are bigger than Surprise Stadium's, which can hold 3,600 fans.

sections 113-118, with Rangers players signing down the right field line and Royals players signing down the left field line.

Players from the Rangers and Royals will sometimes sign after they have been removed from the game as they walk along the warning track back to their respective clubhouses. The best place to be at that time is sections 122 and 124 (Rangers) and sections 121 and 123 (Royals).

FOOD FOR THOUGHT
A handful of specialty concession stands can be found on the concourse down the left field line. The diverse offerings change yearly, but barbeque, funnel cakes, and cheese steaks seem to be a constant.

SODA AND SUDS

Coca-Cola controls the soft drink market, but alcohol choices are numerous, with wine sold by the glass, margaritas served frozen, and at least a half-dozen beers on tap. Not all beers are served at all stands, with one exception: the Beer Garden taps a keg of each. You can find the Beer Garden mixed in with the specialty concession stands.

AREA INFO

Surprise Stadium is the westernmost spring training ballpark in the Phoenix area, found 25 miles northwest of the Arizona capital. Just as the two team complex in neighboring Peoria spurred stadium-centered development, so too is the case in Surprise. But the immediate development surrounding the stadium in Surprise is much more community oriented than in Peoria. Residences, schools, public recreation and service buildings flank different sides of Surprise Stadium, while a Mecca of commerce can be found a short drive away on Bell Road. It all adds up to a perfect mix of live, work, play...and a lot of traffic congestion on game day. So be prepared for stop and go traffic before and after games.

Travelers' notes

- The closest major highway is the Loop 101, about 8 miles away.
- Phoenix Sky Harbor International Airport is 23.5 miles away.
- There are no safety concerns here.

NEARBY HOTELS

Approximate distance (in miles) to the ballpark is listed in parenthesis.

Holiday Inn Express (0.1)
16540 N Bullard Ave
Surprise, AZ 85374
Phone: 623-975-5540

Hampton Inn (2.4)
14783 W Grand Ave
Surprise, AZ 85374
Phone: 623-537-9122

Quality Inn (2.9)
16741 N Greasewood St
Surprise, AZ 85374
Phone: 623-583-3500

Days Inn (2.9)
12477 W Bell Rd
Surprise, AZ 85374
Phone: 623-933-4000

NEARBY RESTAURANTS

Approximate distance (in miles) to the ballpark is listed in parenthesis.

TGI Friday's (1.0)
14127 W Bell Rd
Surprise, AZ 85374
Phone: 623-546-7727

Carrabba's (1.1)
14043 W Bell Rd
Surprise, AZ 85374
Phone: 623-214-3299

Red Robin (1.1)
14015 W Bell Rd
Surprise, AZ 85374
Phone: 623-556-9066

Buffalo Wild Wings (1.3)
13882 W Bell Rd
Surprise, AZ 85374
Phone: 623-584-2323

The Royals will play 18 games in 2011 at Surprise Stadium, where for the second straight spring the Rangers will play 16.

LOOKING BACK AT LAST YEAR

Spring training records were not a harbinger of regular season records to come for Surprise's two teams. The Rangers went 9-18-1 in Arizona, then turned things around and won the AL West with ease in route to their first World Series. The Royals, on the other hand, had a respectable 13-12-4 mark during their time in Arizona then wound up in the AL Central cellar with a 67-95 record.

The Rangers made a marked improvement in attendance at Surprise Stadium, where their 14 home games in 2010 drew an average crowd of 6,465, which was good for 7th in the Cactus League and was a 1,392 per game rise from 2009. Royals home game crowds ranked them 7th in the Cactus League in 2009, but their average crowd decreased by 411 fans in 2010 to 5,283, a number that placed the team 12th in the attendance rankings.

2010 Rangers Home Record: 4-10
Highest Attendance: 8,373 (vs. Diamondbacks on March 14)
Lowest Attendance: 3,993 (vs. Padres on March 12)

2010 Royals Home Record: 7-6-2
Highest Attendance: 7,436 (vs. A's on March 27)
Lowest Attendance: 2,177 (vs. Giants on March 24)

2011 RANGERS HOME SCHEDULE

SUN	MON	TUES	WED	THURS	FRI	SAT
27 Royals	28 Royals	1	2 Angels	3 Indians	4	5
6 Brewers	7	8	9 A's	10 White Sox	11 Reds	12
13 Giants	14 Dodgers	15	16 Rockies	17	18	19 Mariners
20	21	22	23 D-backs	24 Padres	25	26 Cubs
27	28	29	30	31		

The games on March 16 & 24 start at 6:05 p.m.

All other games start at 1:05 p.m. local time.

For the full Rangers spring training schedule, see page 179.

2011 ROYALS HOME SCHEDULE

SUN	MON	TUES	WED	THURS	FRI	SAT
27	28	1 Padres	2	3	4 Cubs	5 Rockies
6	7 D-backs	8 Reds	9	10	11	12 Dodgers
13	14	15 A's	16	17 Mariners	18 Indians	19
20 Rangers	21 Indians	22 Angels	23	24	25 Giants	26
27 Giants	28 Brewers	29 White Sox	30	31		

The games on March 17, 22 & 25 start at 6:05 p.m.

The game on March 29 starts at 12:05 p.m.

All other games start at 1:05 p.m. local time.

For the full Royals spring training schedule, see page 171.

TEMPE DIABLO STADIUM
2200 West Alameda Drive
Tempe, AZ 85282

The 2011 spring training season will be the Angels' 19th in Tempe, where they have a lease to train through 2025.

LOCATION
Tempe Diablo Stadium shares something in common with Angel Stadium in Anaheim: both are adjacent to office complexes and have a stretch of Interstate visible just beyond their outfield wall. Besides 1-10 and office buildings, the stadium is bordered by one of Tempe's Twin Buttes and the practice fields that make up the Angels' 75-acre spring training complex.

DIRECTIONS
Take 1-10 to the Broadway Road exit (#153 from the east or #153-B from the west). Travel west on Broadway to 48th Street and turn left. Travel south on 48th to Alameda Drive and turn left. The stadium is a half-mile ahead on the left.

PARKING
There are two paved parking lots on opposite sides of the stadium. But those 1,350 spaces fill up well before game time. Most people will have to park in one of the lots at the office complexes across the street from the stadium. There will be people to guide you where you need to go.
  Cost: $5

Trivia Tidbit
Tempe Diablo Stadium has been the inaugural spring training home of three teams: the Seattle Pilots (1969), Milwaukee Brewers (1970) and Seattle Mariners (1977).

BALLPARK BASICS
Capacity: 9,558
Opened: 1968
Construction cost: $600,000
Primary architect: DLR Group (2006 renovations)

Owned by the City of Tempe Parks and Recreation Department and operated on game day by the Tempe Diablos.

First game: The Seattle Pilots defeated the Cleveland Indians 19-3 on March 7, 1969 in front of 1,032 fans.

Outfield Dimensions	Phone:
LF: 340' CF: 420' RF: 360'	480-858-7500

BALLPARK OVERVIEW
Tempe Diablo Stadium sits at the base of the Twin Buttes, one of which rises above the left field wall. The rocky hill with an American flag atop provides a stunning backdrop. Fitting given its hillside location, the stadium is built upon a small hill that necessitates fans to access it via stairs or a ramp, making Tempe Diablo Stadium the only non-street level ballpark in the Cactus League. The stadium's picturesque exterior facade is topped by the Angels' halo logo. Inside, pennants from the years the Angels have gone to the playoffs are affixed to the facade of the

press box. The stadium first hosted spring training in 1969 and underwent an extensive $5.9 million renovation to lure the Angels to Tempe in 1993. In 2006, further renovations to the stadium and surrounding complex were completed at a cost of $20 million. Although the stadium itself is architecturally pleasing, its seating bowl features an overabundance of bleachers and all seats are serviced by a cramped concourse, both no-nos by modern-day standards. Games are played on Gene Autry Field, which was named in honor of the original and longtime Angels owner in 1999, the year after he passed away.

Outside the Park
Most fans enter the ballpark through the entrance gates behind home plate. A limited number enter from gates behind first base. Either way, the gates can only be reached by stairs or the handicapped accessible ramps found on either side of the stadium.

Ticket windows are at street level in a building just to the right of the staircases.

Will Call is found at Window 6 (for last names that begin with A-L) and Window 7 (M-Z) in the sole ticket office on stadium property.

Inside the Park
The narrow concourse is open to the playing field and is covered by a trellised roof until it widens and becomes open-air past the third base dugout.

The Angels' bullpen is behind the right field fence, out of sight from fans. The visitors' bullpen is in foul territory down the left field line.

Tempe Diablo Stadium is noted for its scenic butte backdrop.

The stadium's sole scoreboard is in right-center field and features a line score along with basic game information (balls, strikes, outs, name of player at-bat).

The audio system has been completely updated since last spring as a distributed sound system was installed throughout the stadium. In the past, there was just one speaker in center field.

The main Angels team shop is behind first base. A tent set up on the left field concourse also carries plenty of merchandise.

PRACTICE FIELDS

The Angels' practice fields are next door to the stadium, extending from it to 48th Street. During February workouts, the fields are accessible as soon as the Angels start their practice, which is usually around 9:30 a.m. The same fields, however, are off-limits once games begin, when the team takes their pre-game batting practice on the field next to the stadium's west parking lot, where fans can watch from behind a chain link fence that's just beyond the left field wall of the practice field.

146

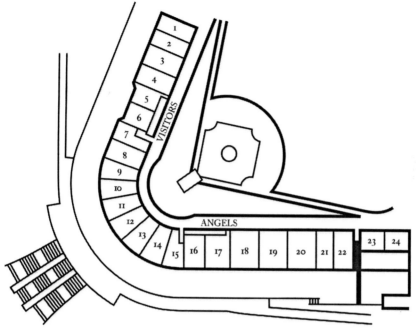

Tempe Diablo Stadium Seating Chart

SEATING

Tempe Diablo Stadium, which can hold 9,558 fans, is one of three ballparks in the Cactus League with a listed capacity of less than 10,000. By a 3,570 to 3,231 count, it has more bleacher seats than stadium seats, but at least all seats in the stadium have backs. Traditional chair back seats with cup holders are between the dugouts, with bleacher benches beyond. A berm on the left half of the stadium can seat up to 2,300.

SECTIONS & TICKET PRICES

Homeplate MVP

Sections 7-15
Seat rows: A-D in all sections
The first four rows of the nine sections between the dugouts.
  Cost: $29

Field MVP

Sections 5-17

Seat rows: E to W in sections 5-7, 9, 13 and 15-17; E to Z in sections 8, 10-12 and 14

Besides the high-end Homeplate MVP, these are the only sections in the stadium with actual seats, which makes them high demand.

Cost: $23

Field Box

Sections 1-4 and 18-22

Seat rows: B to Z in section 1; B to W in sections 2-4 and 18-22

Their name is a misnomer, as the Field Box seats are nothing more than aluminum bleachers. The first four sections are down the left field line while sections 18-22 are along the right field line.

Cost: $16

Grandstand

Sections 23-24

Seat rows: B to K in both sections

These two sections are as far down the right field line as you can get and have much better views of Tempe's Twin Buttes than the Tempe Diablo Stadium diamond.

Cost: $10

Lawn

General Admission

The berm extends from the end of the third base grandstand to the hitters' backdrop in left-center field. Unlike in the rest of the ballpark, fans in the berm have a roomy concourse and easy access to concessions. Considering the inexpensive price of a lawn ticket, that makes a good deal even better.

Cost: $6

Handicapped Seating

Handicap seating is available in platforms at the top of sections 2-7, 9, 13 and 15-22.

VIP seating

The upper level structure next to the press box also houses a handful of suites, which combined can hold up to 60 people.

WHAT YOU NEED TO KNOW BEFORE YOU GO

1. The Angels dugout is on the first base side. To make sure you're on the home side of the stadium, buy your tickets in sections 11-24.
2. There are no rows I, O or Q in any section.
3. The protective netting behind home plate extends from sections 7-15 but is barely noticeable to those sitting behind it.
4. For views of the Twin Butte sit anywhere on the right half (first base side) of the stadium. Seats on the left half provide only views of I-10 and skimpy palm trees as a backdrop.
5. Limited standing room is available on the covered concourse and also on the open-air patio down the left field line.
6. The only thing blocking fans from moving from one section to another are large crowds. Ushers won't.

Seats to avoid

A small handful of seats are partially obstructed by the green metal protruding from the tunnels that are cut into the grandstand. The tunnels are used by the players to access their clubhouses. The seats with obstructions are:

- In section 7: seats 1-4 in row M
- In section 15: seats 9-13 in row M

Seats in the two Grandstand sections (23-24) should only be bought as a last resort. Views from there are blocked by fans standing up in the Field Box sections, which happens when players walk by after they've been removed from the game. Even unobstructed views come at a price, as you'll have to crane your neck to the left for the whole game since the seats face towards the outfield. So given the choice of Grandstand or Lawn seating, choose the berm.

Seats in the shade

Very few. The only shade provided in the roofless stadium's seating sections is cast upon the upper rows primarily on the first base side and comes courtesy of the trellised roof over the concourse. Seats that are in the shade at game's beginning can be found in rows W & up in sections 10-12 and rows V & up in sections 13-22. As the sun slowly descends behind the grandstand during the game shade creeps downward so that rows P & up in sections 10-12 and rows T & up in sections 13-22 are shaded by 2:30.

BUYING TICKETS

There are three ways to purchase tickets for Angels games at Tempe Diablo Stadium:
1. Online at www.angelsbaseball.com.
2. By calling Ticketmaster at **480-784-4444 or 800-745-3000**.
3. In person. Beginning February 12, the stadium's box office is open from 9 a.m. to 5 p.m. on Monday through Friday and 9 a.m. to 4 p.m. on Saturday.

Children

Ages 2 & under get in free and do not require a ticket.

GAME DAY

Gates open approximately an hour and a half before game time, which means 11:30 a.m. for the typical 1:05 p.m. start.

Angel autographs aplenty can be had outside of the stadium, where early arrivals often enjoy close encounters with players in the west parking lot.

Food, drink and bag policy

- Fans can bring water inside, up to one liter per person in a factory sealed plastic bottle. No other beverages are permitted.
- Food is not allowed to be brought into the stadium in bulk quantities. Fruit must be sliced.
- Bags larger than 16" x 16" x 8" are prohibited.

Getting autographs

Tempe is tops in the Cactus League in autograph accessibility. To guarantee you get a slew of signatures from the home team, arrive while the Angels are taking batting practice, which they do exclusively on the field adjacent to the west parking lot. After a group of players has finished hitting they walk from the practice field through the north end of the parking lot to the

151

main stadium. The pathway is lined by a steel barricade only about three feet in height and the majority of players will stop to sign for fans gathered there. For the normal game time (1:05), the best timeframe to gather along the walkway is 11:15 to 11:30.

Inside the stadium, players sign down the outfield lines before the game. Visitors sign down the left field line, between their dugout and end of the grandstand. Angel autographs can be had well down the right field line next to the tunnel between sections 22 and 23. That tunnel leads to the home team clubhouse and is the place to be after the game, as quite a few Angels (players and coaches) will sign near its entrance before continuing into their clubhouse.

FOOD FOR THOUGHT
Specialty food tents are found on the concourse down the left field line, which also features a picnic area and a lookout deck filled with high top bar tables. Unfortunately the choices there and throughout the stadium are fairly routine. The highlight is the supersized portobello mushroom sandwich that comes from the grills on the concourse that also cook burgers, sausages and hot dogs during the game.

SODA AND SUDS
Beverage service is dominated by Pepsi (soft drinks) and Miller Lite (beer). Besides Miller products, there are numerous beers on tap. Recent options have included Foster's and Rolling Rock.

AREA INFO
Tempe Diablo Stadium is synonymous with congestion. The stadium is tightly fit into real estate bordered by a rock formation, industrial section and two traffic-clogged major highways (I-10 and Highway 60). The end result is traffic headaches coming and going, the worst you'll find in spring

The Angels will play 16 games in 2011 at Tempe Diablo Stadium, where they went 6-8-2 in 2010 before an average crowd of 6,940.

training on either coast. Your options are limited to waiting it out. And as inviting as the 25-acre Twin Buttes are, they are off limits to anybody wanting to hike them as they are controlled by a Marriott Resort that has been built into their hillside.

Travelers' notes
- The closest Interstate, I-10, runs parallel to the right field wall.
- Phoenix Sky Harbor International Airport is 4.7 miles away.
- The entire area surrounding the stadium is quite safe. It's hard enough for regular folks to come and go thanks to the traffic. Criminals would have no chance to escape!

NEARBY HOTELS

Approximate distance (in miles) to the ballpark is listed in parenthesis.

Hampton Inn (0.6)
4234 S 48th St
Phoenix, AZ 85040
Phone: 602-438-8688

Comfort Inn (0.7)
1625 S 52nd St
Tempe, AZ 85281
Phone: 480-446-9500

Sheraton (0.75)
1600 S 52nd St
Tempe, AZ 85281
Phone: 480-967-6600

Red Roof Inn (0.8)
2135 W 15th St
Tempe, AZ 85281
Phone: 480-449-3205

NEARBY RESTAURANTS

Approximate distance (in miles) to the ballpark is listed in parenthesis.

Zax Incredible Subs (0.45)
2403 W Huntington Dr
Tempe, AZ 85282
Phone: 602-438-2995

Whataburger (0.5)
4610 S 48th St
Phoenix, AZ 85040
Phone: 602-454-6453

Pizza Hut (0.5)
4708 S 48th St
Phoenix, AZ 85040
Phone: 602-438-9236

China Farm Buffet (0.55)
3135 S 48th St
Tempe, AZ 85282
Phone: 602-438-2707

LOOKING BACK AT LAST YEAR

Just like in the 2010 regular season, which concluded with an 80-82 record, the Angels finished two games below .500 (13-15) during 2010 spring training, which was the direct result of their two games below .500 record at their winter home in Tempe, where they drew an average crowd of 6,940. That marked an

increase of 1,635 per home game from 2009 and ranked the
Angels 5th in average attendance out of the 15 teams that train
in Arizona.

2010 Home Record: 6-8-2
Highest Attendance: 8,911 (vs. Diamondbacks on March 17)
Lowest Attendance: 3,536 (vs. Padres on March 9)

2011 ANGELS HOME SCHEDULE

SUN	MON	TUES	WED	THURS	FRI	SAT
						26 Dodgers
27	28 A's	1 Reds	2	3 Royals	4 White Sox	5
6 D-backs	7	8 Rangers	9 Rockies	10 Royals	11 D-backs	12
13 Mariners	14	15	16	17	18 Padres	19 Indians
20	21 Cubs	22	23 Giants	24 Brewers	25	26

All games start at 1:05 p.m. local time.
For the full Angels spring training schedule, see page 172.

CACTUS LEAGUE MUSEUM

As it enters its 65th season in 2011, the Cactus League has amassed plenty of history while expanding from 2 to 15 teams in a state that was largely unsettled when the Cleveland Indians and New York Giants set up camp in Arizona in 1947.

Since its humble and technically unofficial beginnings (the name "Cactus League" dates to 1954), the Arizona-based spring training circuit has hosted two-thirds of Major League Baseball's current 30 franchises and 14 Arizona cities have had a hand in shaping the Cactus League of today. Eight of those cities continue to host the teams that currently train in the state.

"Play Ball: The Cactus League Experience," an exhibit began by the Mesa Historical Museum in 2009, tells the story of the teams, towns, stadiums and people that have been the fabric of the Cactus League experience.

Much like the league it details, the exhibit has expanded significantly from its modest origins, when about 200 objects occupied 1,000 square feet in a single location, to what it is in 2011: a collection of nearly 800 objects spread out over 5,500 square feet of space in three locations.

Photographs, artwork and artifacts compliment the oral dialogues and well-researched and written historical accounts that collectively tell the Cactus League story.

Artifacts on display range from historical to whimsical. Programs date back to 1946 and include one from Mickey Mantle's rookie year of 1951, when the New York Yankees trained for the first and only time in Arizona following an agreement to swap camps with the Giants, who would later

This home plate came from the field at Francisco Grande where the Giants practiced for two decades. It is one of nearly 800 objects that the Mesa Historical Museum has acquired to tell the story of spring training's history in Arizona.

train for many springs at their Francisco Grande complex in Casa Grande, about 50 miles southeast of Phoenix. A home plate from one of the four long gone fields at Francisco Grande is part of the collection of Cactus League ballpark items at which fans can gawk. Visitors can also gaze upon a cactus signed by Prince Fielder and a grapefruit autographed by Sammy Sosa (then read the story behind the unusual memorabilia). Baseballs signed by greats, like Joe DiMaggio, can also be seen and memorabilia once on display at Scottsdale's legendary Pink Pony Steak House, which for decades served as the Cactus League's unofficial watering hole, has found a place where it can again be appreciated by a baseball adoring public after it was acquired at the estate auction of the Pink Pony's longtime proprietor last summer.

For those wanting to immerse themselves in the complete history of Arizona's annual rite of spring, here's what you need to know and where you need to go:

The Cactus League story is told through exhibits and artifacts at a museum in Tempe run by the Arizona Historical Society.

THE ARIZONA HISTORICAL SOCIETY'S MUSEUM AT PAPAGO PARK

1300 North College Avenue
Tempe, AZ 85281

The entire story of the Cactus League is told here in a year-round exhibit that opens to the public on February 19, 2011 and will continue to be housed at the AHS's Tempe location until March 2013. Over 400 objects are on display. All stadiums, past and present, are featured and a replica dugout is being built into the 3,000 square feet of space that will serve as the primary exhibit space for "The Cactus League Experience."

Admission: $5 for adults, ages 12-18 and 60+ are $4, kids 11 & under are free
Hours: 10 a.m. to 4 p.m. on Tuesday through Saturday; Noon to 4 p.m. on Sunday
Phone: 480-929-9499

The Cubs have long been the Cactus League's most popular team and their spring training history is mixed in with family-friendly interactive activities at Mesa's Arizona Museum for Youth.

ARIZONA MUSEUM FOR YOUTH

35 North Robson Street
Mesa, AZ 85201

In 2010, the entire exhibit was on display here. The focus in 2011 has shifted to the teams that have called Mesa their winter home and the three stadiums that have hosted spring training baseball since the Cubs were the first to arrive in Mesa in 1952. Befitting of a museum's whose purpose is to provide accessible and interactive exhibits for children and families, visitors can make their own baseball card and design a stadium. Over 100 artifacts will be on display from February 25 to August 7 in what is deemed as the "Mesa Plays Ball" portion of the Cactus League Experience.

Admission: $7 for everyone age 2 and over
Hours: 10 a.m. to 4 p.m. on Tuesday through Saturday; Noon to 4 p.m. on Sunday
Phone: 480-644-2468

PHOENIX SKY HARBOR INTERNATIONAL AIRPORT
3400 East Sky Harbor Boulevard
Phoenix, AZ 85034

Most commercial airline passenger traffic at Phoenix's airport is served by Terminal 4 and in the retail area of that terminal is where a 1,000-square foot display catches the attention of passersby with a gallery of baseball art and then educates all-comers to the baseball legends who have trained in Arizona. The primary purpose of the items on display at PHX from February 18 through September 11 is to garner interest for the exhibits found in the museums in Mesa and Tempe.

Admission: Free
Hours: The airport is always open
Phone: 602-273-3300

Eventually, the Mesa Historical Museum hopes to organize all of their collection in a single state-of-the-art museum, with the Cubs' new spring training complex and associated Wrigleyville West development the desired location when both are tentatively set to open in 2013. To increase exposure in the interim, project leaders for what serves as the Cactus League museum have contracted with the entities mentioned above to show and tell the story of the rich history of spring training baseball in Arizona.

2011 CACTUS LEAGUE TEAM SCHEDULES

Note: All times listed are local (based on the stadium where the game is played). Schedules are accurate as of January 23, 2011.

2011 ARIZONA D-BACKS SPRING TRAINING SCHEDULE

Date	Day	Game	Time	Location
Feb. 25	Friday	D-backs at Giants	1:05	Scottsdale
Feb. 26	Saturday	Rockies at D-backs	1:10	Salt River
Feb. 27	Sunday	Giants at D-backs	1:10	Salt River
Feb. 28	Monday	Rockies at D-backs	1:10	Salt River
March 1	Tuesday	D-backs at Rockies	1:10	Salt River
March 2	Wednesday	Mariners at D-backs	1:10	Salt River
March 2	Wednesday	D-backs at Giants	7:05	Scottsdale
March 3	Thursday	D-backs at Padres	1:05	Peoria
March 4	Friday	Padres at D-backs	1:10	Salt River
March 5	Saturday	Rangers at D-backs	1:10	Salt River
March 6	Sunday	D-backs at Angels	1:05	Tempe
March 7	Monday	D-backs at Royals	1:05	Surprise
March 8	Tuesday	D-backs at Indians	1:05	Goodyear
March 9	Wednesday	Brewers at D-backs	1:10	Salt River
March 10	Thursday	White Sox at D-backs	6:40	Salt River
March 11	Friday	D-backs at Angels	1:05	Tempe
March 12	Saturday	D-backs at Brewers	1:05	Maryvale
March 12	Saturday	D-backs at Rockies	6:40	Salt River
March 13	Sunday	Cubs at D-backs	1:10	Salt River
March 14	Monday	Off		
March 15	Tuesday	Giants at D-backs	6:40	Salt River
March 16	Wednesday	Angels at D-backs	1:10	Salt River
March 17	Thursday	D-backs at Dodgers	1:05	Glendale
March 18	Friday	D-backs at Mariners	1:05	Peoria
March 19	Saturday	Reds at D-backs	1:10	Salt River
March 20	Sunday	D-backs at A's	1:05	Phoenix
March 20	Sunday	D-backs at Indians	1:05	Goodyear
March 21	Monday	Dodgers at D-backs	6:40	Salt River
March 22	Tuesday	Indians at D-backs	1:10	Salt River
March 23	Wednesday	D-backs at Rangers	1:05	Surprise
March 24	Thursday	A's at D-backs	1:10	Salt River
March 25	Friday	D-backs at White Sox	7:05	Glendale
March 26	Saturday	Royals at D-backs	1:10	Salt River
March 27	Sunday	D-backs at Reds	1:05	Goodyear
March 28	Monday	Rangers at D-backs	1:10	Salt River
March 29	Tuesday	D-backs at Cubs	1:05	Mesa

2011 CHICAGO CUBS SPRING TRAINING SCHEDULE

Date	Day	Game	Time	Location
Feb. 27	Sunday	A's at Cubs	1:05	Mesa
Feb. 28	Monday	Brewers at Cubs	1:05	Mesa
March 1	Tuesday	Cubs at Giants	1:05	Scottsdale
March 2	Wednesday	Cubs at Brewers	1:05	Maryvale
March 3	Thursday	Rangers at Cubs	1:05	Mesa
March 4	Friday	Cubs at Royals	1:05	Surprise
March 5	Saturday	Padres at Cubs	1:05	Mesa
March 6	Sunday	Dodgers at Cubs	1:05	Mesa
March 6	Sunday	Cubs at Reds	1:05	Goodyear
March 7	Monday	Angels at Cubs	1:05	Mesa
March 8	Tuesday	Cubs at Rockies	1:10	Salt River
March 9	Wednesday	Royals at Cubs	1:05	Mesa
March 10	Thursday	Indians at Cubs	1:05	Mesa
March 11	Friday	Cubs at White Sox	1:05	Glendale
March 12	Saturday	Reds at Cubs	1:05	Mesa
March 12	Saturday	Reds vs. Cubs	1:05	Las Vegas
March 13	Sunday	Dodgers vs. Cubs	1:05	Las Vegas
March 13	Sunday	Cubs at D-backs	1:10	Salt River
March 14	Monday	Cubs at Mariners	1:05	Peoria
March 15	Tuesday	Rockies at Cubs	1:05	Mesa
March 15	Tuesday	Cubs at A's	1:05	Phoenix
March 16	Wednesday	Off		
March 17	Thursday	Cubs at A's	1:05	Phoenix
March 18	Friday	Reds at Cubs	1:05	Mesa
March 19	Saturday	Cubs at Padres	1:05	Peoria
March 20	Sunday	Giants at Cubs	1:05	Mesa
March 21	Monday	Cubs at Angels	1:05	Tempe
March 22	Tuesday	Cubs at Dodgers	1:05	Glendale
March 23	Wednesday	A's at Cubs	1:05	Mesa
March 24	Thursday	White Sox at Cubs	2:05	Mesa
March 25	Friday	Mariners at Cubs	1:05	Mesa
March 26	Saturday	Cubs at Rangers	1:05	Surprise
March 27	Sunday	Rockies at Cubs	1:05	Mesa
March 28	Monday	Cubs at Indians	1:05	Goodyear
March 29	Tuesday	D-backs at Cubs	1:05	Mesa

2011 CHICAGO WHITE SOX SPRING TRAINING SCHEDULE

Date	Day	Game	Time	Location
Feb. 28	Monday	White Sox at Dodgers	1:05	Glendale
March 1	Tuesday	Brewers at White Sox	1:05	Glendale
March 2	Wednesday	White Sox at Reds	1:05	Goodyear
March 3	Thursday	Mariners at White Sox	1:05	Glendale
March 4	Friday	White Sox at Angels	1:05	Tempe
March 5	Saturday	White Sox at Indians	1:05	Goodyear
March 6	Sunday	Royals at White Sox	1:05	Glendale
March 7	Monday	Indians at White Sox	1:05	Glendale
March 8	Tuesday	Rockies at White Sox	1:05	Glendale
March 9	Wednesday	White Sox at Giants	1:05	Scottsdale
March 10	Thursday	White Sox at Rangers	1:05	Surprise
March 10	Thursday	White Sox at D-backs	6:40	Salt River
March 11	Friday	Cubs at White Sox	1:05	Glendale
March 12	Saturday	Rangers at White Sox	1:05	Glendale
March 13	Sunday	White Sox at Dodgers	1:05	Glendale
March 14	Monday	Padres at White Sox	1:05	Glendale
March 15	Tuesday	Off		
March 16	Wednesday	Giants at White Sox	1:05	Glendale
March 17	Thursday	White Sox at Brewers	1:05	Maryvale
March 17	Thursday	White Sox at Rockies	1:10	Salt River
March 18	Friday	A's at White Sox	4:05	Glendale
March 19	Saturday	White Sox at A's	1:05	Phoenix
March 20	Sunday	Dodgers at White Sox	1:05	Glendale
March 21	Monday	White Sox at Padres	7:05	Peoria
March 22	Tuesday	White Sox at Mariners	1:05	Peoria
March 23	Wednesday	Dodgers at White Sox	1:05	Glendale
March 24	Thursday	White Sox at Cubs	2:05	Mesa
March 25	Friday	D-backs at White Sox	7:05	Glendale
March 26	Saturday	Angels at White Sox	1:05	Glendale
March 27	Sunday	White Sox at Brewers	1:05	Maryvale
March 28	Monday	Reds at White Sox	1:05	Glendale
March 29	Tuesday	White Sox at Royals	12:05	Surprise
March 30	Wednesday	White Sox at Dash	6:00	Winston-Salem

2011 CINCINNATI REDS SPRING TRAINING SCHEDULE

Date	Day	Game	Time	Location
Feb. 27	Sunday	Reds at Indians	1:05	Goodyear
Feb. 28	Monday	Indians at Reds	1:05	Goodyear
March 1	Tuesday	Reds at A's	1:05	Phoenix
March 1	Tuesday	Reds at Angels	1:05	Tempe
March 2	Wednesday	White Sox at Reds	1:05	Goodyear
March 3	Thursday	Dodgers at Reds	7:05	Goodyear
March 4	Friday	Reds at Mariners	1:05	Peoria
March 5	Saturday	Reds at Dodgers	1:05	Glendale
March 6	Sunday	Cubs at Reds	1:05	Goodyear
March 7	Monday	Brewers at Reds	1:05	Goodyear
March 8	Tuesday	Reds at Royals	1:05	Surprise
March 9	Wednesday	Reds at Padres	1:05	Peoria
March 10	Thursday	Giants at Reds	1:05	Goodyear
March 11	Friday	Reds at Rangers	1:05	Surprise
March 12	Saturday	Reds at Cubs	1:05	Mesa
March 12	Saturday	Reds vs. Cubs	1:05	Las Vegas
March 13	Sunday	Angels at Reds	1:05	Goodyear
March 14	Monday	Reds at Rockies	1:10	Salt River
March 15	Tuesday	Off		
March 16	Wednesday	Royals at Reds	7:05	Goodyear
March 17	Thursday	Indians at Reds	1:05	Goodyear
March 18	Friday	Reds at Cubs	1:05	Mesa
March 19	Saturday	Rockies at Reds	1:05	Goodyear
March 19	Saturday	Reds at Diamondbacks	1:10	Salt River
March 20	Sunday	Reds at Brewers	1:05	Maryvale
March 21	Monday	Mariners at Reds	1:05	Goodyear
March 22	Tuesday	A's at Reds	1:05	Goodyear
March 23	Wednesday	Reds at Padres	1:05	Peoria
March 24	Thursday	Rangers at Reds	1:05	Goodyear
March 25	Friday	Padres at Reds	1:05	Goodyear
March 26	Saturday	Reds at Giants	3:10	Scottsdale
March 27	Sunday	Diamondbacks at Reds	1:05	Goodyear
March 28	Monday	Reds at White Sox	1:05	Glendale
March 29	Tuesday	Reds at Indians	12:05	Goodyear

2011 CLEVELAND INDIANS SPRING TRAINING SCHEDULE

Date	Day	Game	Time	Location
Feb. 27	Sunday	Reds at Indians	1:05	Goodyear
Feb. 28	Monday	Indians at Reds	1:05	Goodyear
March 1	Tuesday	Dodgers at Indians	1:05	Goodyear
March 2	Wednesday	Indians at A's	1:05	Phoenix
March 3	Thursday	Indians at Rangers	1:05	Surprise
March 4	Friday	Rockies at Indians	1:05	Goodyear
March 5	Saturday	White Sox at Indians	1:05	Goodyear
March 5	Saturday	Indians at Mariners	1:05	Peoria
March 6	Sunday	Indians at Rockies	1:10	Salt River
March 7	Monday	Indians at White Sox	1:05	Glendale
March 8	Tuesday	D-backs at Indians	1:05	Goodyear
March 9	Wednesday	Padres at Indians	1:05	Goodyear
March 10	Thursday	Indians at Cubs	1:05	Mesa
March 11	Friday	Mariners at Indians	1:05	Goodyear
March 12	Saturday	Angels at Indians	2:05	Goodyear
March 13	Sunday	Indians at Padres	1:05	Peoria
March 14	Monday	A's at Indians	1:05	Goodyear
March 15	Tuesday	Brewers at Indians	1:05	Goodyear
March 16	Wednesday	Off		
March 17	Thursday	Indians at Reds	1:05	Goodyear
March 18	Friday	Indians at Royals	1:05	Surprise
March 18	Friday	Rangers at Indians	7:05	Goodyear
March 19	Saturday	Indians at Angels	1:05	Tempe
March 20	Sunday	D-backs at Indians	1:05	Goodyear
March 21	Monday	Indians at Royals	1:05	Surprise
March 22	Tuesday	Indians at D-backs	1:10	Salt River
March 23	Wednesday	Royals at Indians	1:05	Goodyear
March 24	Thursday	Indians at Giants	7:05	Scottsdale
March 25	Friday	Indians at Brewers	1:05	Maryvale
March 26	Saturday	Giants at Indians	7:05	Goodyear
March 27	Sunday	Indians at Dodgers	1:05	Glendale
March 28	Monday	Cubs at Indians	1:05	Goodyear
March 29	Tuesday	Reds at Indians	12:05	Goodyear
March 30	Wednesday	Indians at Clippers	1:05	Columbus

2011 COLORADO ROCKIES SPRING TRAINING SCHEDULE

Date	Day	Game	Time	Location
Feb. 26	Saturday	Rockies at D-backs	1:10	Salt River
Feb. 27	Sunday	Off		
Feb. 28	Monday	Rockies at D-backs	1:10	Salt River
March 1	Tuesday	D-backs at Rockies	1:10	Salt River
March 2	Wednesday	Rockies at Padres	1:05	Peoria
March 3	Thursday	Giants at Rockies	1:10	Salt River
March 4	Friday	Rockies at Indians	1:05	Goodyear
March 5	Saturday	Rockies at Royals	1:05	Surprise
March 6	Sunday	Indians at Rockies	1:10	Salt River
March 7	Monday	Dodgers at Rockies	1:10	Salt River
March 8	Tuesday	Rockies at White Sox	1:05	Glendale
March 8	Tuesday	Cubs at Rockies	1:10	Salt River
March 9	Wednesday	Rockies at Angels	1:05	Tempe
March 10	Thursday	Rockies at Brewers	1:05	Maryvale
March 11	Friday	Royals at Rockies	1:10	Salt River
March 12	Saturday	Padres at Rockies	1:10	Salt River
March 12	Saturday	D-backs at Rockies	6:40	Salt River
March 13	Sunday	Rockies at A's	1:05	Phoenix
March 14	Monday	Reds at Rockies	1:10	Salt River
March 15	Tuesday	Rockies at Cubs	1:05	Mesa
March 16	Wednesday	Rockies at Rangers	6:05	Surprise
March 17	Thursday	White Sox at Rockies	1:10	Salt River
March 18	Friday	Brewers at Rockies	1:10	Salt River
March 19	Saturday	Rockies at Reds	1:05	Goodyear
March 20	Sunday	Angels at Rockies	1:10	Salt River
March 21	Monday	Rockies at Giants	1:05	Scottsdale
March 22	Tuesday	Off		
March 23	Wednesday	Mariners at Rockies	6:40	Salt River
March 24	Thursday	Rockies at Dodgers	1:05	Glendale
March 25	Friday	Rangers at Rockies	6:40	Salt River
March 26	Saturday	Rockies at A's	7:05	Phoenix
March 27	Sunday	Rockies at Cubs	1:05	Mesa
March 27	Sunday	A's at Rockies	1:10	Salt River
March 28	Monday	Rockies at Mariners	1:05	Peoria
March 29	Tuesday	Mariners at Rockies	1:10	Salt River
March 30	Wednesday	Rockies at Drillers	6:05	Tulsa, OK

2011 KANSAS CITY ROYALS SPRING TRAINING SCHEDULE

Date	Day	Game	Time	Location
Feb. 27	Sunday	Royals at Rangers	1:05	Surprise
Feb. 28	Monday	Royals at Rangers	1:05	Surprise
March 1	Tuesday	Padres at Royals	1:05	Surprise
March 2	Wednesday	Royals at Dodgers	1:05	Glendale
March 3	Thursday	Royals at Angels	1:05	Tempe
March 4	Friday	Cubs at Royals	1:05	Surprise
March 5	Saturday	Rockies at Royals	1:05	Surprise
March 6	Sunday	Royals at White Sox	1:05	Glendale
March 7	Monday	D-backs at Royals	1:05	Surprise
March 7	Monday	Royals at Padres	7:05	Peoria
March 8	Tuesday	Reds at Royals	1:05	Surprise
March 9	Wednesday	Royals at Cubs	1:05	Mesa
March 10	Thursday	Royals at A's	1:05	Phoenix
March 10	Thursday	Royals at Angels	1:05	Tempe
March 11	Friday	Royals at Rockies	1:10	Salt River
March 12	Saturday	Dodgers at Royals	1:05	Surprise
March 13	Sunday	Royals at Brewers	1:05	Maryvale
March 14	Monday	Off		
March 15	Tuesday	A's at Royals	1:05	Surprise
March 16	Wednesday	Royals at Reds	7:05	Goodyear
March 17	Thursday	Mariners at Royals	6:05	Surprise
March 18	Friday	Indians at Royals	1:05	Surprise
March 19	Saturday	Royals at Giants	1:05	Scottsdale
March 20	Sunday	Rangers at Royals	1:05	Surprise
March 21	Monday	Indians at Royals	1:05	Surprise
March 22	Tuesday	Angels at Royals	6:05	Surprise
March 23	Wednesday	Royals at Indians	1:05	Goodyear
March 24	Thursday	Royals at Mariners	1:05	Peoria
March 25	Friday	Giants at Royals	6:05	Surprise
March 26	Saturday	Royals at D-backs	1:10	Salt River
March 27	Sunday	Giants at Royals	1:05	Surprise
March 28	Monday	Brewers at Royals	1:05	Surprise
March 29	Tuesday	White Sox at Royals	12:05	Surprise

2011 LOS ANGELES ANGELS SPRING TRAINING SCHEDULE

Date	Day	Game	Time	Location
Feb. 26	Saturday	Dodgers at Angels	1:05	Tempe
Feb. 27	Sunday	Angels at Dodgers	1:05	Glendale
Feb. 28	Monday	A's at Angels	1:05	Tempe
March 1	Tuesday	Reds at Angels	1:05	Tempe
March 2	Wednesday	Angels at Rangers	1:05	Surprise
March 3	Thursday	Royals at Angels	1:05	Tempe
March 4	Friday	White Sox at Angels	1:05	Tempe
March 5	Saturday	Angels at Brewers	1:05	Maryvale
March 6	Sunday	D-backs at Angels	1:05	Tempe
March 7	Monday	Angels at Cubs	1:05	Mesa
March 8	Tuesday	Rangers at Angels	1:05	Tempe
March 9	Wednesday	Rockies at Angels	1:05	Tempe
March 10	Thursday	Royals at Angels	1:05	Tempe
March 10	Thursday	Angels at Mariners	1:05	Peoria
March 11	Friday	D-backs at Angels	1:05	Tempe
March 12	Saturday	Angels at Indians	2:05	Goodyear
March 13	Sunday	Mariners at Angels	1:05	Tempe
March 13	Sunday	Angels at Reds	1:05	Goodyear
March 14	Monday	Off		
March 15	Tuesday	Angels at Padres	1:05	Peoria
March 16	Wednesday	Angels at D-backs	1:10	Salt River
March 17	Thursday	Angels at Giants	7:05	Scottsdale
March 18	Friday	Padres at Angels	1:05	Tempe
March 19	Saturday	Indians at Angels	1:05	Tempe
March 20	Sunday	Angels at Rockies	1:10	Salt River
March 21	Monday	Cubs at Angels	1:05	Tempe
March 22	Tuesday	Angels at Royals	6:05	Surprise
March 23	Wednesday	Giants at Angels	1:05	Tempe
March 24	Thursday	Brewers at Angels	1:05	Tempe
March 25	Friday	Angels at A's	1:05	Phoenix
March 26	Saturday	Angels at White Sox	1:05	Glendale
March 27	Sunday	Padres at Angels	2:05	Anaheim
March 28	Monday	Angels at Dodgers	7:10	Los Angeles
March 29	Tuesday	Dodgers at Angels	7:05	Anaheim

2011 LOS ANGELES DODGERS SPRING TRAINING SCHEDULE

Date	Day	Game	Time	Location
Feb. 26	Saturday	Dodgers at Angels	1:05	Tempe
Feb. 26	Saturday	Dodgers at Giants	1:05	Scottsdale
Feb. 27	Sunday	Angels at Dodgers	1:05	Glendale
Feb. 28	Monday	White Sox at Dodgers	1:05	Glendale
March 1	Tuesday	Dodgers at Indians	1:05	Goodyear
March 2	Wednesday	Royals at Dodgers	1:05	Glendale
March 3	Thursday	Dodgers at Reds	7:05	Goodyear
March 4	Friday	Giants at Dodgers	7:05	Glendale
March 5	Saturday	Reds at Dodgers	1:05	Glendale
March 6	Sunday	Dodgers at Cubs	1:05	Mesa
March 7	Monday	Dodgers at Rockies	1:10	Salt River
March 8	Tuesday	Dodgers at Brewers	1:05	Maryvale
March 9	Wednesday	Mariners at Dodgers	1:05	Glendale
March 10	Thursday	Padres at Dodgers	1:05	Glendale
March 11	Friday	Dodgers at A's	1:05	Phoenix
March 12	Saturday	Dodgers at Royals	1:05	Surprise
March 12	Saturday	Dodgers at Giants	1:05	Scottsdale
March 13	Sunday	White Sox at Dodgers	1:05	Glendale
March 13	Sunday	Dodgers vs. Cubs	1:05	Las Vegas
March 14	Monday	Dodgers at Rangers	1:05	Surprise
March 15	Tuesday	Rangers at Dodgers	1:05	Glendale
March 16	Wednesday	Off		
March 17	Thursday	D-backs at Dodgers	1:05	Glendale
March 18	Friday	Dodgers at Giants	1:05	Scottsdale
March 19	Saturday	Brewers at Dodgers	1:05	Glendale
March 20	Sunday	Dodgers at White Sox	1:05	Glendale
March 21	Monday	A's at Dodgers	1:05	Glendale
March 21	Monday	Dodgers at D-backs	6:40	Salt River
March 22	Tuesday	Cubs at Dodgers	1:05	Glendale
March 23	Wednesday	Dodgers at White Sox	1:05	Glendale
March 24	Thursday	Rockies at Dodgers	1:05	Glendale
March 25	Friday	Dodgers at Mariners	7:05	Peoria
March 26	Saturday	Dodgers at Padres	1:05	Peoria
March 27	Sunday	Indians at Dodgers	1:05	Glendale
March 28	Monday	Angels at Dodgers	7:10	Los Angeles
March 29	Tuesday	Dodgers at Angels	7:05	Anaheim
March 30	Wednesday	Mariners at Dodgers	7:05	Los Angeles

2011 MILWAUKEE BREWERS SPRING TRAINING SCHEDULE

Date	Day	Game	Time	Location
Feb. 28	Monday	Giants at Brewers	1:05	Maryvale
Feb. 28	Monday	Brewers at Cubs	1:05	Mesa
March 1	Tuesday	Brewers at White Sox	1:05	Glendale
March 2	Wednesday	Cubs at Brewers	1:05	Maryvale
March 3	Thursday	A's at Brewers	1:05	Maryvale
March 4	Friday	Brewers at Giants	1:05	Scottsdale
March 5	Saturday	Angels at Brewers	1:05	Maryvale
March 6	Sunday	Brewers at Rangers	1:05	Surprise
March 6	Sunday	Brewers at A's	1:05	Phoenix
March 7	Monday	Brewers at Reds	1:05	Goodyear
March 8	Tuesday	Dodgers at Brewers	1:05	Maryvale
March 9	Wednesday	Brewers at D-backs	1:10	Salt River
March 10	Thursday	Rockies at Brewers	1:05	Maryvale
March 11	Friday	A's at Brewers	1:05	Maryvale
March 12	Saturday	D-backs at Brewers	1:05	Maryvale
March 13	Sunday	Royals at Brewers	1:05	Maryvale
March 14	Monday	Brewers at Giants	1:05	Scottsdale
March 15	Tuesday	Brewers at Indians	1:05	Goodyear
March 16	Wednesday	Brewers at Mariners	7:05	Peoria
March 17	Thursday	White Sox at Brewers	1:05	Maryvale
March 18	Friday	Brewers at Rockies	1:10	Salt River
March 19	Saturday	Brewers at Dodgers	1:05	Glendale
March 20	Sunday	Reds at Brewers	1:05	Maryvale
March 21	Monday	Rangers at Brewers	1:05	Maryvale
March 22	Tuesday	Padres at Brewers	1:05	Maryvale
March 23	Wednesday	Off		
March 24	Thursday	Brewers at Angels	1:05	Tempe
March 25	Friday	Indians at Brewers	1:05	Maryvale
March 26	Saturday	Mariners at Brewers	1:05	Maryvale
March 27	Sunday	White Sox at Brewers	1:05	Maryvale
March 28	Monday	Padres at Brewers	1:05	Maryvale
March 28	Monday	Brewers at Royals	1:05	Surprise
March 29	Tuesday	Brewers at Padres	12:05	Peoria

2011 OAKLAND A'S SPRING TRAINING SCHEDULE

Date	Day	Game	Time	Location
Feb. 27	Sunday	A's at Cubs	1:05	Mesa
Feb. 28	Monday	A's at Angels	1:05	Tempe
March 1	Tuesday	Reds at A's	1:05	Phoenix
March 2	Wednesday	Indians at A's	1:05	Phoenix
March 3	Thursday	A's at Brewers	1:05	Maryvale
March 4	Friday	Rangers at A's	1:05	Phoenix
March 5	Saturday	Giants at A's	1:05	Phoenix
March 6	Sunday	Brewers at A's	1:05	Phoenix
March 6	Sunday	A's at Padres	1:05	Peoria
March 7	Monday	Mariners at A's	1:05	Phoenix
March 8	Tuesday	Padres at A's	1:05	Phoenix
March 9	Wednesday	A's at Rangers	1:05	Surprise
March 10	Thursday	Royals at A's	1:05	Phoenix
March 11	Friday	Dodgers at A's	1:05	Phoenix
March 11	Friday	A's at Brewers	1:05	Maryvale
March 12	Saturday	A's at Mariners	1:05	Peoria
March 13	Sunday	Rockies at A's	1:05	Phoenix
March 14	Monday	A's at Indians	1:05	Goodyear
March 15	Tuesday	Cubs at A's	1:05	Phoenix
March 15	Tuesday	A's at Royals	1:05	Surprise
March 16	Wednesday	Off		
March 17	Thursday	Cubs at A's	1:05	Phoenix
March 18	Friday	A's at White Sox	4:05	Glendale
March 19	Saturday	White Sox at A's	1:05	Phoenix
March 20	Sunday	Diamondbacks at A's	1:05	Phoenix
March 20	Sunday	A's at Giants	1:05	Scottsdale
March 21	Monday	A's at Dodgers	1:05	Glendale
March 22	Tuesday	A's at Reds	1:05	Goodyear
March 23	Wednesday	A's at Cubs	1:05	Mesa
March 24	Thursday	A's at Diamondbacks	1:10	Salt River
March 25	Friday	Angels at A's	1:05	Phoenix
March 26	Saturday	Rockies at A's	7:05	Phoenix
March 27	Sunday	A's at Rockies	1:10	Salt River
March 28	Monday	A's at Giants	1:05	San Francisco
March 29	Tuesday	Giants at A's	7:05	Oakland
March 30	Wednesday	A's at Giants	12:45	San Francisco

2011 SAN DIEGO PADRES SPRING TRAINING SCHEDULE

Date	Day	Game	Time	Location
Feb. 27	Sunday	Padres at Mariners	1:05	Peoria
Feb. 28	Monday	Mariners at Padres	1:05	Peoria
March 1	Tuesday	Padres at Royals	1:05	Surprise
March 2	Wednesday	Rockies at Padres	1:05	Peoria
March 3	Thursday	D-backs at Padres	1:05	Peoria
March 4	Friday	Padres at D-backs	1:10	Salt River
March 5	Saturday	Padres at Cubs	1:05	Mesa
March 6	Sunday	A's at Padres	1:05	Peoria
March 7	Monday	Royals at Padres	7:05	Peoria
March 8	Tuesday	Padres at A's	1:05	Phoenix
March 9	Wednesday	Reds at Padres	1:05	Peoria
March 9	Wednesday	Padres at Indians	1:05	Goodyear
March 10	Thursday	Padres at Dodgers	1:05	Glendale
March 11	Friday	Giants at Padres	7:05	Peoria
March 12	Saturday	Padres at Rockies	1:10	Salt River
March 13	Sunday	Indians at Padres	1:05	Peoria
March 14	Monday	Padres at White Sox	1:05	Glendale
March 15	Tuesday	Angels at Padres	1:05	Peoria
March 16	Wednesday	Off		
March 17	Thursday	Rangers at Padres	7:05	Peoria
March 18	Friday	Padres at Angels	1:05	Tempe
March 19	Saturday	Cubs at Padres	1:05	Peoria
March 20	Sunday	Padres at Mariners	1:05	Peoria
March 21	Monday	White Sox at Padres	7:05	Peoria
March 22	Tuesday	Padres at Brewers	1:05	Maryvale
March 23	Wednesday	Reds at Padres	1:05	Peoria
March 24	Thursday	Padres at Rangers	6:05	Surprise
March 25	Friday	Padres at Reds	1:05	Goodyear
March 26	Saturday	Dodgers at Padres	1:05	Peoria
March 27	Sunday	Padres at Angels	2:05	Anaheim
March 28	Monday	Padres at Brewers	1:05	Maryvale
March 29	Tuesday	Brewers at Padres	12:05	Peoria

176

2011 SAN FRANCISCO GIANTS SPRING TRAINING SCHEDULE

Date	Day	Game	Time	Location
Feb. 25	Friday	D-backs at Giants	1:05	Scottsdale
Feb. 26	Saturday	Dodgers at Giants	1:05	Scottsdale
Feb. 27	Sunday	Giants at D-backs	1:10	Salt River
Feb. 28	Monday	Giants at Brewers	1:05	Maryvale
March 1	Tuesday	Cubs at Giants	1:05	Scottsdale
March 2	Wednesday	D-backs at Giants	7:05	Scottsdale
March 3	Thursday	Giants at Rockies	1:10	Salt River
March 4	Friday	Brewers at Giants	1:05	Scottsdale
March 4	Friday	Giants at Dodgers	7:05	Glendale
March 5	Saturday	Giants at A's	1:05	Phoenix
March 6	Sunday	Mariners at Giants	1:05	Scottsdale
March 7	Monday	Rangers at Giants	7:05	Scottsdale
March 8	Tuesday	Giants at Mariners	1:05	Peoria
March 9	Wednesday	White Sox at Giants	1:05	Scottsdale
March 10	Thursday	Giants at Reds	1:05	Goodyear
March 11	Friday	Giants at Padres	7:05	Peoria
March 12	Saturday	Dodgers at Giants	1:05	Scottsdale
March 13	Sunday	Giants at Rangers	1:05	Surprise
March 14	Monday	Brewers at Giants	1:05	Scottsdale
March 15	Tuesday	Giants at D-backs	6:40	Salt River
March 16	Wednesday	Giants at White Sox	1:05	Glendale
March 17	Thursday	Angels at Giants	7:05	Scottsdale
March 18	Friday	Dodgers at Giants	1:05	Scottsdale
March 19	Saturday	Royals at Giants	1:05	Scottsdale
March 20	Sunday	A's at Giants	1:05	Scottsdale
March 20	Sunday	Giants at Cubs	1:05	Mesa
March 21	Monday	Rockies at Giants	1:05	Scottsdale
March 22	Tuesday	Off		
March 23	Wednesday	Giants at Angels	1:05	Tempe
March 24	Thursday	Indians at Giants	7:05	Scottsdale
March 25	Friday	Giants at Royals	6:05	Surprise
March 26	Saturday	Reds at Giants	3:10	Scottsdale
March 26	Saturday	Giants at Indians	7:05	Goodyear
March 27	Sunday	Giants at Royals	1:05	Surprise
March 28	Monday	A's at Giants	1:05	San Francisco
March 29	Tuesday	Giants at A's	7:05	Oakland
March 30	Wednesday	A's at Giants	12:45	San Francisco

2011 SEATTLE MARINERS SPRING TRAINING SCHEDULE

Date	Day	Game	Time	Location
Feb. 27	Sunday	Padres at Mariners	1:05	Peoria
Feb. 28	Monday	Mariners at Padres	1:05	Peoria
March 1	Tuesday	Rangers at Mariners	1:05	Peoria
March 2	Wednesday	Mariners at D-backs	1:10	Salt River
March 3	Thursday	Mariners at White Sox	1:05	Glendale
March 4	Friday	Reds at Mariners	1:05	Peoria
March 5	Saturday	Indians at Mariners	1:05	Peoria
March 6	Sunday	Mariners at Giants	1:05	Scottsdale
March 7	Monday	Mariners at A's	1:05	Phoenix
March 8	Tuesday	Giants at Mariners	1:05	Peoria
March 9	Wednesday	Mariners at Dodgers	1:05	Glendale
March 10	Thursday	Angels at Mariners	1:05	Peoria
March 11	Friday	Mariners at Indians	1:05	Goodyear
March 12	Saturday	A's at Mariners	1:05	Peoria
March 13	Sunday	Mariners at Angels	1:05	Tempe
March 14	Monday	Cubs at Mariners	1:05	Peoria
March 15	Tuesday	Off		
March 16	Wednesday	Brewers at Mariners	7:05	Peoria
March 17	Thursday	Mariners at Royals	6:05	Surprise
March 18	Friday	D-backs at Mariners	1:05	Peoria
March 19	Saturday	Mariners at Rangers	1:05	Surprise
March 20	Sunday	Padres at Mariners	1:05	Peoria
March 21	Monday	Mariners at Reds	1:05	Goodyear
March 22	Tuesday	White Sox at Mariners	1:05	Peoria
March 23	Wednesday	Mariners at Rockies	6:40	Salt River
March 24	Thursday	Royals at Mariners	1:05	Peoria
March 25	Friday	Mariners at Cubs	1:05	Mesa
March 25	Friday	Dodgers at Mariners	7:05	Peoria
March 26	Saturday	Mariners at Brewers	1:05	Maryvale
March 27	Sunday	Rangers at Mariners	1:05	Peoria
March 28	Monday	Rockies at Mariners	1:05	Peoria
March 29	Tuesday	Mariners at Rockies	1:10	Salt River
March 30	Wednesday	Mariners at Dodgers	7:05	Los Angeles

2011 TEXAS RANGERS SPRING TRAINING SCHEDULE

Date	Day	Game	Time	Location
Feb. 27	Sunday	Royals at Rangers	1:05	Surprise
Feb. 28	Monday	Royals at Rangers	1:05	Surprise
March 1	Tuesday	Rangers at Mariners	1:05	Peoria
March 2	Wednesday	Angels at Rangers	1:05	Surprise
March 3	Thursday	Indians at Rangers	1:05	Surprise
March 3	Thursday	Rangers at Cubs	1:05	Mesa
March 4	Friday	Rangers at A's	1:05	Phoenix
March 5	Saturday	Rangers at D-backs	1:10	Salt River
March 6	Sunday	Brewers at Rangers	1:05	Surprise
March 7	Monday	Rangers at Giants	7:05	Scottsdale
March 8	Tuesday	Rangers at Angels	1:05	Tempe
March 9	Wednesday	A's at Rangers	1:05	Surprise
March 10	Thursday	White Sox at Rangers	1:05	Surprise
March 11	Friday	Reds at Rangers	1:05	Surprise
March 12	Saturday	Rangers at White Sox	1:05	Glendale
March 13	Sunday	Giants at Rangers	1:05	Surprise
March 14	Monday	Dodgers at Rangers	1:05	Surprise
March 15	Tuesday	Rangers at Dodgers	1:05	Glendale
March 16	Wednesday	Rockies at Rangers	6:05	Surprise
March 17	Thursday	Rangers at Padres	7:05	Peoria
March 18	Friday	Rangers at Indians	7:05	Goodyear
March 19	Saturday	Mariners at Rangers	1:05	Surprise
March 20	Sunday	Rangers at Royals	1:05	Surprise
March 21	Monday	Rangers at Brewers	1:05	Maryvale
March 22	Tuesday	Off		
March 23	Wednesday	D-backs at Rangers	1:05	Surprise
March 24	Thursday	Rangers at Reds	1:05	Goodyear
March 24	Thursday	Padres at Rangers	6:05	Surprise
March 25	Friday	Rangers at Rockies	6:40	Salt River
March 26	Saturday	Cubs at Rangers	1:05	Surprise
March 27	Sunday	Rangers at Mariners	1:05	Peoria
March 28	Monday	Rangers at D-backs	1:10	Salt River
March 29	Tuesday	Rangers at Coastal Carolina	6:35	Myrtle Beach
March 30	Wednesday	Rangers at Express	6:30	Round Rock

179

SCHEDULE OF CACTUS LEAGUE NIGHT GAMES

For those hoping to see two games in one day, this is the schedule you need. There are 28 games that start after 6:00 p.m. on the 2011 Cactus League schedule. Given that all ten of Arizona's spring training ballparks are within 50 miles of each other, enjoying a day/night doubleheader on the 17 days that the schedule makes it possible isn't really difficult.

Date	Day	Game	Time	Location
March 2	Wednesday	D-backs at Giants	7:05	Scottsdale
March 3	Thursday	Dodgers at Reds	7:05	Goodyear
March 4	Friday	Giants at Dodgers	7:05	Glendale
March 7	Monday	Royals at Padres	7:05	Peoria
March 7	Monday	Rangers at Giants	7:05	Scottsdale
March 10	Thursday	White Sox at D-backs	6:40	Salt River
March 11	Friday	Giants at Padres	7:05	Peoria
March 12	Saturday	D-backs at Rockies	6:40	Salt River
March 15	Tuesday	Giants at D-backs	6:40	Salt River
March 16	Wednesday	Rockies at Rangers	6:05	Surprise
March 16	Wednesday	Royals at Reds	7:05	Goodyear
March 16	Wednesday	Brewers at Mariners	7:05	Peoria
March 17	Thursday	Mariners at Royals	6:05	Surprise
March 17	Thursday	Rangers at Padres	7:05	Peoria
March 17	Thursday	Angels at Giants	7:05	Scottsdale
March 18	Friday	Rangers at Indians	7:05	Goodyear
March 21	Monday	Dodgers at D-backs	6:40	Salt River
March 21	Monday	White Sox at Padres	7:05	Peoria
March 22	Tuesday	Angels at Royals	6:05	Surprise
March 23	Wednesday	Mariners at Rockies	6:40	Salt River
March 24	Thursday	Padres at Rangers	6:05	Surprise
March 24	Thursday	Indians at Giants	7:05	Scottsdale
March 25	Friday	Giants at Royals	6:05	Surprise
March 25	Friday	Rangers at Rockies	6:40	Salt River
March 25	Friday	D-backs at White Sox	7:05	Glendale
March 25	Friday	Dodgers at Mariners	7:05	Peoria
March 26	Saturday	Rockies at A's	7:05	Phoenix
March 26	Saturday	Giants at Indians	7:05	Goodyear

ACKNOWLEDGEMENTS

I would like to thank the following people for their assistance in helping me obtain the seating chart diagrams that were used in this book:

Amanda Broadway, Jeff Overton and Jonathan Vasquez (Camelback Ranch)
Natalie Naples (Goodyear Ballpark)
Mark Gallo and Dyan Seaburg (Hohokam Park)
Chris Shaheen (Maryvale Baseball Park)
Jennifer Loper (Peoria Sports Complex)
Travis LoDolce and James Vujs (Phoenix Municipal Stadium)
Levi Long (Salt River Fields)
Jeff Cesaretti and Jason Waldron (Scottsdale Stadium)
Clint Freeman and Kendra Lyons (Surprise Stadium)
Jerry Hall and Cynthia Yanez (Tempe Diablo Stadium)

Additionally, I would like to thank:

Levi Long, again, for the architectural renderings of Salt River Fields.

Lisa Anderson, the executive director of the Mesa Historical Museum, which is responsible for "Play Ball: The Cactus League Experience," for filling me in on the details about the current and future plans for their Cactus League exhibit.

All of the ushers and other stadium personnel, most of whom volunteer their time through their local civic organizations, for answering my questions about their ballparks and cities.

ABOUT THE AUTHOR

Graham Knight lives in Georgia, the state from which he has embarked 11 times to enjoy the springtime version of our national pastime. One of those journeys, made as a much younger fan, resulted in him getting an opportunity to be the bat boy for the Boston Red Sox, his favorite team. He's been hooked on spring training ever since.

After eight trips to Florida, Graham finally made it to Arizona in 2008 for spring training and returned to the Grand Canyon State again in 2009 as part of his ambitious quest to see a game in every Cactus and Grapefruit League ballpark over the course of one spring training. That trip inspired this book, the first edition of which was his first.

A 1999 graduate of the University of Georgia, Graham has put his journalism degree to use primarily by writing, editing and organizing content for the World Wide Web, starting with major market FOX TV Web sites and including a six year stint as the online director for a baseball training aids and instruction Web site.

Since 2002, Graham has operated BaseballPilgrimages.com, where he has written over 75 detailed ballpark articles. Shortly after his first son, Zachary, was born in November of 2008, he launched SpringTrainingConnection.com. This book is an expanded version of what's found online there.

The author of this book, Graham Knight, holds up a copy of its first edition during a 2010 Cactus League game at Mesa's Hohokam Park.

LaVergne, TN USA
29 March 2011
222069LV00012B/172/P